PLANT
THIS
INSTEAD!

First published in 2014 by Cool Springs Press,
an imprint of the Quayside Publishing Group,
400 First Avenue North, Suite 400, Minneapolis, MN 55401

The information in this book is true and complete to the best
of our knowledge. All recommendations are made without any
guarantee on the part of the author or Publisher, who also
disclaims any liability incurred in connection with the use of
this data or specific details.

Cool Springs Press titles are also available at discounts
in bulk quantity for industrial or sales promotional use. For
details write to Special Sales Manager at Cool Springs Press,
400 First Avenue North, Suite 400, Minneapolis, MN 55401 USA.
To find out more about our books, visit us online at
www.coolspringspress.com.

Library of Congress Cataloging-in-Publication Data
Marden, Troy B.
    Plant this instead! : better plant choices :
prettier · hardier · blooms longer · new colors · less work ·
drought-tolerant · native / Troy B. Marden.
    pages cm
    Includes index.
    ISBN 978-1-59186-576-6 (softcover)
    1. Landscape plants. 2. Landscape gardening. I. Title.

SB407.M2544 2014
635.9--dc23
            2013032504

Acquisitions Editor: Billie Brownell
Design Manager: Cindy Samargia Laun
Design and layout: Diana Boger
Cover Design: John Barnett

Printed in China
10 9 8 7 6 5 4 3 2 1

PLANT THIS INSTEAD!

BETTER PLANT CHOICES

Prettier • Hardier • Blooms Longer • New Colors • Less Work • Drought-Tolerant • Native

TROY B. MARDEN

COOL SPRINGS PRESS

Home and Garden Experts™

MINNEAPOLIS, MINNESOTA

Dedication

This book is dedicated to my aunt,
Maureen "Budgie" Marden. She showed all of us
how to love the simplest things in life.

Acknowledgments

To Jerome—Thank you for your patience and
for making me smile every day.

To Billie—Thank you for your unending support,
your perseverance on this project, and for making
me look better than I really am. Thanks also to
Cool Springs Press for your faith in this book.

A special thanks to Cheekwood Botanical Garden
for letting me show up with my camera, usually
unannounced, at all hours of the day and night,
and especially on Mondays.

Contents

INTRODUCTION

Have you ever walked through your local garden center or nursery, looking out across the vast sea of choices before you and wondered, how will I ever decide what to plant? Have you hired a landscaper or landscape designer and questioned whether their recommendations for your yard were the best varieties for you to grow? Were they just offering you what they had on hand at the time? What about thumbing through those catalogs that begin showing up in the mailbox in late winter and early spring, enticing you with "glamour shots" of plants that you seemingly can't live without? Will they really thrive in your yard or garden? These questions and more are what *Plant This Instead!* will help you answer.

In the 1980s, the Bradford pear rose to horticultural superstardom as a fast-growing, tidy, and disease-resistant tree whose white spring blooms and saturated, long-lasting red fall color were the most desirable of ornamental traits. Thirty years later, those trees are splitting in half under the weight of ice and snow, losing large limbs in windstorms, and damaging homes, cars, and more in the process. Once touted as a "fruitless" ornamental, Bradford and other varieties of callery pear are now reseeding with wild abandon in forested areas, choking out native vegetation and disrupting local ecosystems. Yet they are still being sold—but there are vastly better choices.

The Bradford pear is but one example on a long list of plants in today's nurseries and garden centers that have proven problematic in the landscape for a variety of reasons. In a few cases, they may truly be aggressive or invasive in nature, but the opposite can also be true. Perhaps they are weak or lacking in vigor. Maybe they are prone to attacks by insects or susceptible to outbreaks of difficult-to-control diseases. Today's conscientious gardeners are working hard to be less dependent on chemical sprays, so plants with natural resistance to pests and diseases are increasingly popular, and for good reason. Less spraying is not only safer for the environment as a whole, but it is better for the smaller ecosystems that exist within

our gardens, too—and it's safer for us, the gardeners. Other maintenance factors play into our decisions, too, and when we are considering new plants, tasks such as pruning, watering, fertilizing, staking, and others must be taken into account. The less of this we have to do, the lower maintenance our gardens become, and as we trend toward smaller landscapes and gardens, high-maintenance, disease-prone, invasive, or aggressive plants are simply not feasible.

Plant This Instead! offers suggestions for replacing these and a wide range of other trees, shrubs, flowering plants, and vines whose landscape value is often questionable. It also addresses the many advances that have been made in plant breeding, especially in annual and perennial garden flowers, in the past two decades. Plants once thought of as utilitarian have been reinvented with new colors, more vigor, and improved hardiness, and instead of being supporting characters, they now take starring roles in many beds and borders.

Where appropriate, *Plant This Instead!* proposes native plants as replacements for nonnative and invasive species, but this isn't a book aimed solely at native plants. Many of our favorite garden and landscape plants, from ginkgo trees to camellias and daylilies, are not part of our native plant palette. This doesn't make them any less valuable or desirable in the garden, and, in fact, with a little knowledge about which varieties are the most useful, they'll mix and mingle in perfect landscape harmony. Occasionally, you'll even run across a native plant that offers beautiful blooms, colorful foliage, or other desirable traits, but when you put it in good garden soil with regular feeding and watering, it becomes a garden thug, running roughshod over nearby plants and all but eliminating anything in its path. *Plant This Instead!* proffers suitable replacements for those as well.

In the following pages, you will find insiders' tips about choosing plant varieties that are appropriate to your climate whether you garden in Zone 3 or Zone 9. What about lawns? Should you have one? What are your options? Are there lower-maintenance alternatives that are more environmentally friendly? You'll learn how to navigate the nursery industry and find plants beyond the standard fare offered in many garden centers today or those recommended by the majority of landscapers and designers. Choosing the right location for a plant is just as important for its survival as choosing the right variety, and there are plenty of hints along those lines, too, all while planting for the future, ensuring healthy environments and ecosystems for generations to come. The focus of the book, though, is dedicated to the plants themselves— perusing, learning, choosing, and growing the plants that will thrive in your garden.

Whether you're a seasoned gardener or a relative newcomer, you'll find inspiration and options galore in the chapters ahead, and with any luck you'll come across something completely new that will grace your garden with its blooms, its fall color, or its beautiful architecture for many years to come.

THE STATE OF OUR LANDSCAPE
(and What Landscapers Don't Tell You)

Our American landscape has become a little boring over the past twenty or so years. We've gotten busy! Everyone works, the kids are involved in activities too numerous to count, and most of the time, weekends are given over to sports, school activities, and other demands rather than leisurely spending the days (or at least *one* day!) in our yards and gardens like our parents and grandparents did before us. Life is different now, but that doesn't mean we can't make beautiful spaces to live in and enjoy—it just means we have to be smarter about how we create them. When we're smart about that, the real work becomes easier. So, here are a few tips and tricks of the trade.

Landscape Designers and Architects

The best ones are those who want to work *with* you to create a space that reflects your own desires and needs and the needs of your family, whether you are a young single in your first home, a couple with children whose needs and schedules take up the majority of your free time, or if you're retired and ready to enjoy life and reap the benefits of working hard for so many years. This is *your* story to tell and *your* outdoor space to create and enjoy, so be sure to find a willing partner who will help you realize your wishes in a way that is greater than you might be able to do on your own.

What Is a "Low-Maintenance" Landscape?

"Low maintenance" has become the catchphrase of the new millennium. "I want a low-maintenance yard," everyone says. The problem with that is what is low maintenance to you might not be low maintenance to me—or to your landscaper or designer, if you have one helping you. We don't really know what "low maintenance" means. Does that mean you don't want to have to water as often? Does it mean you don't want to have to deadhead the flowers? Does it mean you want to keep tasks such as pruning and weeding to a minimum? Or does it mean that—be honest now—you really don't

The quality of the plants you purchase will have a bearing on how well they perform once they are planted in your landscape. It is hard to pass up a "good deal" on a plant that is deeply discounted, but be sure to consider the health, vigor, and viability of that plant before you purchase—or before you let someone sell it to you. Will it thrive once you get it home? If it doesn't, you will be starting over from the beginning when it comes time to replace it, which means waiting additional months or even years for it to reach maturity.

want to ever set foot outdoors? All of those prior questions can be answered. That last one? Well, perhaps it's time for urban living and a nice flat on the 14th floor.

Should I Go All Native?

Plants that are native to the region of the country where you live do have certain advantages when it comes to being well adapted to your local soil and climate. Going all native, though, takes a certain type of person and a definite state of mind. It also takes some compromise because sometimes there simply isn't a native option that will look the same or perform the same function in your landscape as a nonnative plant. In the end, it's all about choosing the right plant for the right place, which will be addressed in detail coming up.

They're Trying to Sell Me an Irrigation System!

When well built and used properly, irrigation systems are an excellent form of insurance for keeping plants alive during periods of heat and drought or when you're away from home. They are also highly abused, being run too frequently and for too short a time (often at the recommendation of the "professionals"), wetting only the surface of the soil and causing landscape plants and lawns to keep all of their roots in the top layers of soil and mulch instead of reaching deep down into the soil to find water. Then, when drought strikes and water restrictions go in place, your irrigation systems are turned off and your plants die.

Getting the Best Plants

If you're using a landscape contractor for the large pieces of your landscape, don't be afraid to ask to see samples of smaller

Landscape or garden designers are often helpful for both big picture ideas and when it comes to pulling all of the finer details of the garden together. The way plants mix and mingle together, as well as with the architectural features of the garden, such as walkways, fences, arbors, and more, will make the difference between a good garden and a great one. An experienced designer can help pull these details together.

Don't be sold on plants that won't thrive in your climate. Study and learn about the plants you wish to grow or that are being recommended to you by your designer or architect. Hopefully, if you've hired a professional to assist you, they will know the best plants for your area, but that isn't always the case. Educate yourself. Check and recheck the list of recommended plants and be sure that what is recommended will thrive where you live.

plants or pictures of the larger ones so that you know what you're paying for and that it's of good quality. If you're shopping on your own, spring and fall will be when nurseries and garden centers have the highest quality plants on their shelves and on their lots. Midsummer may get you some deals, but be sure that the plants are still in good health. Getting 50 percent off on a plant that is dying anyway is only costing you money and delaying success. Usually, it's better to pay a little more for a good, healthy plant that will establish quickly and grow right away rather than to keep replacing half-dead plants that cost you valuable time and money to nurse back to health.

Avoiding the Pitfalls

Let's face it. In nearly every industry there are those hardworking folks who just want to make a good, honest living; support their families; and bring a little happiness to the world along the way and there are those folks who, well, just want to make some money at your expense. The landscaping and gardening industry is no different. Here are a few suggestions on how to avoid having the wool pulled over your eyes.

Don't use a landscaper who says, "We don't need a plan. I have some plants I can bring you." That translates directly to: "I have some plants left over from my last job that I'd love to sell you. They've only been sitting around my garage for a few weeks and I've watered them when I remembered to." More than likely, it also means that you're going to get the same old cheap, cookie-cutter plants that this landscaper uses on every other job they do, with no thought as to whether or not those plants will actually thrive on your site, which brings me to my next point.

Don't settle for plants—from anyone— if you're unsure they will grow in the location they're being recommended for.

Do your research. It's up to you to educate yourself at least a little bit, and even if you're working with a well-respected professional, don't take everything they say as gospel. Once you have a plan in front of you, spend some time looking up the plants they've recommended on the Internet or in a good reference book. If you live in Zone 5 and they're recommending plants that are only hardy to Zone 7, that's a red flag! Do they know what they're doing? Don't be duped.

Know who you are hiring. There are a lot of people out there—men and women— who think that just because they know how to dig a hole, it suddenly makes them a landscape professional. Now, there are many, *many* good self-taught landscapers out there, but there are just as many who wouldn't know a petunia from a pine tree if it jumped up and bit them in the back side. Get references and ask whomever you're hiring to take you to one of their jobsites and let you see their work. If they're good and really know what they're doing, they'll gladly arrange that for you if they want your business.

You say you're ready to do some landscaping? Let's get started! Is this a do-it-yourself project or have you hired a landscape designer, landscape architect, or garden consultant to help you along? Either way is perfectly fine, but let's be realistic, the choices out there before you are vast. When you're faced with all of those choices and decisions, will you just take the easy way out? Will you just plant the same thing your neighbors have in their yard? Or will you take a stand and differentiate yourself from the other homes in the neighborhood? Hopefully, by picking up this book, you've shown an interest in taking a stand—in doing something a little different and making better choices than Bob down the street or Joanne over on the other corner . . . because better plant choices are out there.

RIGHT PLANT, RIGHT PLACE

Considering Your Options and Choosing Your Plants

W hen it comes to choosing plants for landscapes and gardens, it all boils down to one simple task: *choosing the right plant for the right place*. Well, maybe that doesn't sound so simple, but with a little knowledge and guidance from resources like this one and some input from friends who garden, a staff person at your local garden center, or other landscape professionals, you *can* make good choices when it comes to selecting the plants you want to grow and where you want to grow them.

Every plant has a native habitat—a place where it grows naturally or "in the wild," if you will. Understanding a plant's native habitat, whether it's in the open field just behind your house, on the side of a mountain next to a running stream somewhere in China, or in the full sun in an African desert, will help you make the right choice when it comes to selecting the right place for it in your landscape. First, you need to be sure that the plant you want to grow is actually hardy where you live. But what does "hardy" mean? It can mean a lot of things, but when we're talking about plants, it usually refers to a plant's ability to survive the winter in your climate, wherever that may be. For instance, palm trees that thrive on the coast of Florida probably won't last long outdoors after the first frost in Chicago.

It's just too cold and they are not winter hardy.

USDA Hardiness Zones

The USDA (U.S. Department of Agriculture), through many years of research, has come up with a hardiness zone map, which, while not perfect, is extremely helpful for gardeners trying to determine which plants to include in their landscapes. You simply look at the map, figure out which hardiness zone you live in, and then choose plants that are winter hardy to at *least* your zone or colder. The coldest zones, of course, are farther north and are represented by the smallest numbers—Zone 2, for instance—and as you travel south or west into the warmer regions of the country, the numbers increase. Zone 9, for instance, runs along the Gulf Coast and other coastal regions, as well as parts of the West and Southwest. Most plant labels or reference materials will list a plant's hardiness zones. Once you know which zone you live and garden in, you'll have a basic guide to which plants might grow well for you, or at least will survive your winters.

Understanding Your Soil

There are entire books dedicated to soil, and it can be a complicated subject. For most homeowners, the question boils down to whether your soil fits into one of three broad categories: **sand**, **loam**, or **clay**. Sandy soils tend to lose water and dry out very quickly and retain very few nutrients, so watering and fertilizing is key to plants thriving in them. Those blessed with good loam are the luckiest gardeners because loam is just the right combination of sand and clay, but with plenty of organic matter that makes the soil rich and water retentive, yet porous and well drained. Water, nutrients, and air are exchanged freely in loamy soil and plants thrive. Then there is clay, the bane of every gardener's existence. Clay is the smallest particle of soil, with jagged edges that lock together like puzzle pieces, excluding water and air and binding nutrients so tightly that a plant's roots are unable to pull them away. Without water, air, and nutrients readily available to their roots, plants soon begin to struggle and may die if the situation becomes dire enough.

Both clay soils and sandy ones should be amended with large quantities of good **organic matter** such as **compost**, **well-composted manure**, **decaying leaves**, and so forth. Organic matter will improve the water and nutrient-holding capacity of sandy soils, and it will help to loosen

tight clay so that water, air, and nutrients can reach the plants' roots. Even good loam should be replenished regularly with organic matter so that the soil's microbes and its physical structure are well maintained.

When choosing plants for your landscape, further consideration must be given to sun and shade, as well as the microclimates that exist in every yard.

The Question of Sun and Shade

Sun and shade come in varying degrees, but for the purposes of this book, we'll break it down into four basic categories: **full sun**, **part sun**, **part shade**, and **shade**.

Full sun can be defined as any part of your yard that receives more than six

Captivating combinations of foliage provide color and texture in the garden even when plants are not in bloom. This is especially true in shadier nooks where foliage reigns supreme. Here, golden bleeding heart, *Dicentra spectabilis* 'Gold Heart', mingles with false Solomon's seal, *Maianthemum racemosum*, the two complementing each other both in texture and color well into the summer and long after each has finished flowering.

Having success in the garden is all about choosing the right plant for the right place. Plants such as the whale's tongue century plant, *Agave ovatifolia*, are native to dry regions with desert-like climates. In colder climates, where century plants may not grow, winter-hardy plants such as yucca make perfect substitutes.

hours of direct, uninterrupted sun each day (for example, from 7 a.m. until 1 p.m. without the shade of any overhead trees or nearby buildings).

Part sun is defined as any part of the yard that receives four to six hours of sun each day, but may be shaded at certain times. Many gardening books reference plants that do well with "morning sun." This is another way of saying that a plant thrives in part sun.

Part shade is an area of your yard that receives some sun during the day, but it is limited to less than four hours of direct sun. It may also be the very bright shade under a high tree canopy— dappled shade, if you will—where sunlight streams through but is broken by overhead branches and leaves.

Shade is any part of the garden that receives little or no direct sun, but is still light enough for certain plants to grow. It can be found under denser tree canopies that cast even shadows across the ground throughout the day or alongside buildings—especially the north side— where ambient light is present, but direct sun never shines. Shade can be divided into further degrees, but that is beyond the scope of this discussion.

Microclimates

Microclimates are just what the word indicates they are—tiny climates. These are found all around your house and yard, and even within your garden. Buildings create microclimates, larger plants create microclimates, and some microclimates, like those created by a north winter wind, exist naturally. In some Southern gardens, for instance, homeowners may have success with shrubs such as lilacs, which typically don't thrive in the South, if they place them where cold winter winds prevail. Gardeners up north can

use the south side of the house to take advantage of winter sun and warmer microclimates to grow plants that might not be as winter hardy.

Choosing Your Plants

Until you understand how hardiness, soil, light requirements, and microclimates all affect your plant choices, you can choose plants all day long and they may not thrive where you want them to grow. Armed with this knowledge, you can now choose plants based on the part of the country where you live and your basic soil type.

Now for a word on actually *choosing* good plants when you visit the nursery or garden center: choose plants that have an overall healthy appearance. Good plants sit tight in their pots (or rootballs, if you're buying trees or shrubs that are balled-and-burlapped) and have good color— usually green unless a plant is grown for its colored foliage. Whatever the color, it should be bright, clean, and vibrant. If there are brown patches or if the color is off somehow (pale or grayish), the plants may be stressed or otherwise unhealthy. Also look for spots, white patches, or rings on the leaves that may indicate fungal diseases, as well as any insect pests that may be tagging along.

On small plants—annuals and perennials, in particular—don't be afraid to inspect their roots. Turn the pot upside down. Can you see healthy, vigorous, white roots through the holes in the bottom of the pot? You should. Gently push your finger down into the soil in the top of the pot. Is the plant so rootbound that you can't get your finger into the soil? If a plant is that rootbound, it's going to need a little extra TLC when you plant it, cutting through a few of those roots with a sharp knife to encourage new ones to grow out into the soil.

Finally, look for the plants that appear to be part of the most recent shipments. In spring, this is rarely a problem because retailers are selling plants so fast that new shipments are arriving almost daily. As the season progresses, though, and business slows down, those plants will sit on the shelf longer before they are sold and their health and well being are entirely at the mercy of the staff that cares for them. The less time they've spent on the shelf, the more likely they are to thrive once you get them home.

Now that you have a basic understanding of selecting good plants for your landscape, let's talk about planning for their long-term use and the future of your garden.

Annuals and biennials are important in every garden. The seasonal color and interest they provide is indispensible, and while there is some associated cost with adding new plants each year, they provide longer seasons of bloom than almost any perennials. Many, such as foxgloves, *Digitalis purpurea*, will reseed themselves throughout the garden for many seasons.

PLANTING FOR THE LONG-TERM
Investing in the Future of Your Landscape

Landscapes are an investment. In the beginning, they are an investment in time and money to have them designed and installed. As time goes on, they continue to be an investment in care and maintenance, sometimes by your own hand and sometimes by the hand of others. Like all good investments, though, your landscape will pay you back. A well-designed and maintained landscape will add to the monetary value of your home. Should you ever decide to sell your home, a beautiful landscape will add to its asking price and to (hopefully!) the profit that you realize from its sale.

Aside from the obvious financial aspect, a beautiful garden or landscape is also an investment in your personal happiness and well being. You are building your sanctuary when you build your landscape. It makes home a more welcome place to come to for you, your family, and your friends. Whether it's playing host to a weekend barbecue for the neighborhood or the solitude on the back deck with your early morning coffee, your landscape will be the place where you relax, unwind, and have fun. If you build it well and enjoy it, it will repay you many times over in many ways.

Consider, then, planting for the long-term. Not much that we do these days in our consumerist society is truly for the long-term. We drive fast, we eat fast, we talk fast; we move around our world at a frenetic pace, barely finishing one task

Trees are one of the longest-term investments you will make in your landscape. They will provide beauty and shade for generations to come, forming the framework around which the rest of your landscape and garden will be built.

Even in a garden that is comprised mostly of annuals and perennials, planning for the long-term is important. Flowering shrubs and some evergreens may form the bones of the garden and their ultimate size will need to be considered. Perennials will continue to grow larger each year as well. Proper planting and spacing from the beginning will ensure that the garden grows lush and full, but keep plants from crowding one another out.

Arbors and pergolas provide permanent structures for plants growing long-term in the garden. Large perennial vines such as confederate jasmine, *Trachelospermum jasminoides*, can serve a variety of purposes, including softening the hard lines of the structures, providing overhead shade, and supplying spectacular and fragrant floral displays.

before we're on to the next. When you really think about it, we don't even build our own homes for the truly long-term. It wasn't always that way. Certainly, there are plenty of historic neighborhoods with historic homes all across our country, but rarely do we think about the future that is well out ahead of us, perhaps even after we're gone.

With landscaping and especially with the planning for and planting of trees and even some shrubs, it is important to think of the long-term since the tree we plant today will likely not mature in our own lifetime. It will grow and we will revel in its beauty as it does, but a good tree will continue to stand for at least one generation beyond our own and perhaps many. Even if we do think within our own lifetime, tearing out and redoing the landscaping every five to ten years is not only something we *don't* want to do, but it's counterproductive. By constantly tearing out and redoing, the landscape never matures and its true beauty is never realized. The goal in creating any landscape plan, whether on paper or not, should be to design and implement a plan that suits your home for its entire life and matures to a size that fits that home and the land that surrounds it. In order to do this, you must be able to see and think into the future.

Plants grow. We all know this. But when we head out to the nursery or garden center, they just look so small. It's hard to imagine that the 6-foot-tall sugar maple in the 7-gallon nursery container will eventually be a 75-foot-tall tree with a 90-foot spread, but it will! It won't happen tomorrow or the next day or even

next month, next year, or in ten years, but in the future, assuming that it doesn't meet an untimely demise, it will grow that large.

"By the time it gets that large, it will be someone else's problem," you might think to yourself, but why knowingly create a problem for someone else when the best answer is to simply choose the right plant for the right place in the first place.

It is no different with shrubs, when the tiny forsythia at the corner of the garage looks so lonely when it is newly planted, never letting on that in five years' time it will have reached its mature size of 6 feet tall by 8 feet wide! Wise choices backed by a little research mean endless pleasure and enjoyment from your landscape instead of endless work trying to make plants thrive and grow that were doomed to failure from the very beginning. With a lot of planning and a little hard work, your landscape will continue to work for you well into your own future and possibly beyond.

Now, let's talk about plants!

CHAPTER 1

Perennials— Garden Aggressors

Gardeners are often surprised when popular plants that come highly recommended by trusted garden centers and knowledgeable friends suddenly begin a belligerent march across their gardens, running roughshod over nearby plants and encroaching on or even choking out their less-assertive neighbors. These "garden aggressors" can quickly overrun a small garden and even in larger spaces may prove problematic enough to warrant their extraction. Perhaps the better decision is not to include them in the first place. To that end, this chapter explains which plants can be invasive or aggressive in the garden and what suitable alternatives are available.

Garden aggressors are not limited to exotic species from other parts of the world, even though those plants shoulder most of the blame when it comes to complaints of plants being invasive and undesirable. Some of our most popular native perennials, though perfectly suited to their wild habitats, may become monsters when planted in well-prepared garden soil, watered often, and fertilized regularly. The well-informed gardener can make choices regarding which of these they may or may not want to include in their gardens and, with the information in the following pages, can seek out some of the best alternatives to plants that simply may be too aggressive for you to abide.

In some cases, a different species or variety of the same plant may provide the perfect, noninvasive alternative. For others, an entirely different plant may be the better choice. Why not substitute a poorly behaved plant or one whose performance is less desirable with one that will thrill you with its beautiful flowers, gorgeous foliage, or striking architectural form? Here, these options and more are explored to help you make the best possible selection for your own garden, your own climate, and the requirements you need each plant in your garden to fulfill.

Plant This!

Beebalms (*Monarda didyma*) have long been popular garden plants, and rightly so. Properly managed, they make beautiful garden specimens that are hardy, resilient, and show-stopping when in bloom. However, the same characteristics that make them tough and resilient also make them aggressive when it comes to planting them in the garden. Beebalm, like its cousins peppermint and spearmint, has the ability to take over an enormous area of valuable garden real estate in a very short period of time. Its roots are shallow and not difficult to remove, but they do require some management. And, like its other cousins the hyssops, if it's treated too well—good soil and plenty of fertilizer—it tends to become leafy and green at the expense of flowers. Soft, leafy growth is also more susceptible to powdery mildew, an inherent and often frustrating problem.

Eastern Beebalm

A closely related, but often overlooked beebalm is *Monarda fistulosa*, **wild bergamot.** Flowers are light lavender to white with the newer flower stems growing out of the older flowers, giving a unique candelabra effect to the blooms. Where it's happy, it may reach 5 feet in height and while it still may be better suited to restored prairies or wild lands, it is worth consideration by gardeners going for a looser and wilder effect in their garden. Offered by some native plant specialists and several online mail-order nurseries, it deserves to be much more widely known and grown. Not often grown, but closely related and worth mentioning is *Monarda bradburiana*, the **eastern beebalm.** Known almost solely by native plant enthusiasts, it is worth a second look by gardeners due to its greater drought tolerance and exceptional resistance to powdery mildew. Native in much of the central United States from Iowa south to Texas and east at least to Tennessee, it is a noninvasive clump former reaching 18 to 24 inches high by 4 feet wide. The light pink flowers are borne beginning in May, continuing on for several weeks. It is nearly impervious to powdery mildew, even in the hot and humid Southeast.

A number of "mildew-resistant" cultivars are available through nurseries, garden centers, and a variety of online sources. I find that mildew resistance in beebalms has as much to do with spring and early summer weather conditions as it does with specific varieties and their supposed mildew resistance. Even the most resistant varieties will get powdery mildew when conditions are perfect for its growth.

■ **Spreading species** can be kept in check with regular division. Suggested alternates are less invasive and more disease resistant. Attractive to butterflies and desirable pollinators.
■ **FULL SUN.** ■ **ZONES 4 TO 8.**

COMMON GOLDENROD

Plant This!

'Fireworks' Goldenrod

Of the standard goldenrods, **'Fireworks'**, a selection of *Solidago rugosa* bred at the North Carolina Botanical Garden, is one of the best. Less spreading than most, it can be mixed with other perennials without fear of it becoming invasive, though it does form large clumps over time and will need occasional dividing. Flowering earlier than many goldenrods, 'Fireworks' begins its show in late summer on strong, upright stems, with later species carrying the display on into autumn.

Common goldenrod (*Solidago canadensis*) is a denizen of roadsides across America and unfortunately bears the brunt of the blame for causing hay fever and other late summer and autumn allergies, when it is ragweed that is really to blame! As a garden plant, it has several inherent problems, the worst of which is that it is a rampant spreader, quickly colonizing any bit of open soil with its dense and impenetrable roots. Like many plants mentioned in this chapter, it will waste little time invading and eventually choking out the most desirable plants in the garden. That said, a number of garden-worthy hybrids—created mostly by enterprising German plant breeders—and a few well-behaved species do exist. Those with noninvasive habits are worthy additions to the late summer and autumn display.

■ **Goldenrods perform best** in full sun in humusy, well-drained soils with some moisture at their roots. Care should be used in selection to ensure that noninvasive forms are planted. Goldenrod is not the cause of hay fever but often takes the blame for ragweed, which blooms at the same time. ■ **FULL SUN.** ■ **ZONES 3 TO 9.**

Seaside Goldenrod

Other noteworthy species include *Solidago sempervirens*, the **seaside goldenrod**, and *Solidago caesia*, the **wreath** or **zigzag goldenrod**. The former is a tall species, reaching 4 to 6 feet in height, but it has strong stems that remain upright and bear dense, one-sided clusters of showy blooms in September and October. Its strict clumping habit and deep-growing roots make it a desirable and durable selection for the sunny garden. The latter is one of the most unusual and desirable of the goldenrods, with its distinctive wavy or zigzag stems in deep reddish purple that bear golden yellow flowers along much of their length. Also a well-behaved clump former, it draws much attention and many questions from admirers when it's in bloom.

Also of note is ***Solidago sphacelata* 'Golden Fleece'**, an introduction from the Mount Cuba Center in Delaware, which has become extremely popular for the late summer and autumn seasons. Its rounded leaves lend a more refined appearance to the plant and the sprays of golden yellow flowers can be show-stopping. Quite different from most goldenrods, it is worth searching out and trying.

COMMON YARROW

Plant This!

Common yarrow, *Achillea millefolium*, is a popular and widely grown perennial. Its tough constitution and ease of culture makes it a popular choice for unsuspecting beginning gardeners who soon find it running amok through their garden beds, its fleshy underground roots choking out more desirable plants. Where warm summer nights prevail, flowering stems rarely stand upright, their flopping habit making the plant look weedy and unkempt. Since common yarrow regenerates from root cuttings, digging and removing the plants when they become undesirable only leads to more plants and more invasion. Its bad habits, in this gardener's opinion, outweigh its desirable traits. Instead, explore planting several closely related yarrows whose growth habit, richly colored blooms, and similar ease of culture make them perfect substitutes.

'Moonshine' Yarrow

While not a new plant, **'Moonshine' yarrow** is one of the best substitutes for its more aggressive counterpart, common yarrow. Its silver-green, ferny foliage forms the perfect foil for the flat heads of lemon yellow flowers that appear from June through September. It pairs perfectly with the bright and bold colors of the summer garden but is soft and pure enough to mix well with subtler blues, pinks, and whites if those shades are more to your liking. It makes an outstanding and long-lasting cut flower and can also be dried. In the hot and humid Deep South, some gardeners treat **'Moonshine'** as an annual, enjoying its early summer display and replacing it with more heat- and humidity-tolerant plants for late summer and fall displays.

■ **Divide clumps** every two years to maintain vigor and control size. Yarrow makes an excellent cut flower, both fresh and dried. To dry, cut at peak of color and hanging upside down in a warm, dry room. **Drought tolerant once established.**
■ **FULL SUN.** ■ **ZONES 3 TO 8.**

'Appleblossom' Yarrow

If it's the red or pink range of blooms that attracts you to common yarrow, search out the **Galaxy hybrids** when looking for plants to add to your garden. **'Appleblossom' ('Apfelblute')** is one of the most popular, its sturdy, 3-foot stems bearing large, flat heads of peach to salmon-pink flowers, often creating an outstanding dual-tone effect as the flowers age. **'The Beacon' ('Fanal')** sports flowers in a rich shade of brick red with bright yellow centers, standing stiffly upright without falling over, and the flowers of **'Salmon Beauty'** are glowing, salmon-pink blossoms borne in large and very showy heads atop strong stems reaching 3 feet tall.

GARLIC CHIVES

Plant This!

Because young seedlings are nearly identical to, and frequently confused with, common culinary chives (onion chives) in garden centers, many gardeners unknowingly purchase and plant this rampant reseeder, not realizing their mistake until it is too late. There are several distinguishing features between **garlic chives** (*Allium tuberosum*) and their more desirable counterparts, most notably their exceptionally pungent garlicky aroma when the leaves are picked or crushed. Mature foliage is also flat, as opposed to the hollow, tubular leaves of common chives, and garlic chive flowers are white and occur in August instead of the pink springtime blooms of common chives. While garlic chives can be ornamental, deadheading is an absolute must to prevent them taking over.

Common Chives

Common or **onion chives**, *Allium schoenoprasum*, are what most gardeners desire for use in cooking as well as for their ornamental (and edible!) spring flowers. Planted in full sun and well-draining soil, they will remain perennial for many years and provide many meals' worth of delicately onion-flavored leaves, useful in flavoring soups, stews, and other dishes or as a fresh, green garnish where subtle onion flavor might be desirable. **'Forescate'** bears rosy pink blooms on vigorous plants that are about one-third larger in all respects than their traditional counterpart. It is particularly showy when in bloom in April and May.

Blue Skies German Garlic

If their edible quality is of less importance to you, **'Blue Skies' German garlic**, *Allium senescens* 'Blue Skies', is an outstanding ornamental onion growing 18 inches tall and bearing lilac-blue flowers in midsummer. Well-behaved, it only occasionally reseeds, and the few extras are always welcome fillers to transplant and tuck between other plants. Another popular form of the same species, the **"cowlick" allium**, *Allium senescens* 'Glaucum', is a dwarf form with silvery blue leaves that are dramatically twisted and curled.

■ Many species are **beautiful, well-behaved, and garden-worthy.** Those growing from bulbs need a dry period in summer. The smaller-growing species and varieties make excellent additions to a rock garden. Winter foliage is sometimes present, adding ornamental interest. ■ **FULL SUN**. ■ **ZONES 3 TO 8.**

GOOSENECK LOOSESTRIFE

An old-fashioned garden perennial and, in some parts of the country, a favorite passalong plant, **gooseneck loosestrife** (*Lysimachia clethroides*) can and will wreak havoc in most gardens. Spreading viciously by deep and intractable roots, it will make its way across the garden in two seasons or less, running roughshod over, under, and through whatever is in its way. To eradicate it, roots must be completely removed from the soil or they will resprout. In the northern states, cold winters may keep it more in check and cooler summers prolong its flowering, the showy white blooms borne in long, curved or bent spires. In the southern states, the blooms are generally fleeting and the plant quickly takes on a weedy appearance, not offering much in the way of garden interest after its two-week flowering period ends.

Plant This!

'Icicle' Spike Speedwell

White long-leaf veronica (also called spike speedwell), **Veronica longifolia 'Icicle'**, makes an excellent and well-behaved substitute for gooseneck loosestrife. One of the better white-flowering veronicas, it grows 18 to 24 inches tall and flowers from early summer through autumn if deadheaded regularly. In the North, it will remain attractive throughout the growing season, while in the South, a hard cutting back in late summer will encourage a new flush of growth and autumn blooms. A close cousin, **Veronica spicata 'Snow White'**, bears long, branching spikes of white flowers on 18-inch stems in midsummer.

■ **Regular deadheading** will encourage prolonged flowering. Cut back hard in late summer to rejuvenate plants for new growth and fall blooms. Veronica is **a long-lasting cut flower** for summertime arrangements. ■ **FULL TO PART SUN.** ■ **ZONES 3 TO 9.**

Culver's Root

An outstanding native substitute for gooseneck loosestrife is **culver's root**, *Veronicastrum virginicum*. Growing taller than loosestrife, it should be sited appropriately, but it will reward you with a spectacular and welcome show in late summer when, particularly in southern gardens, little may be happening. It performs well in a wide variety of climates from Zones 4 through 8. Many people make the mistake of planting culver's root in shade, but it is most at home in partial to full sun in rich, moist soil, where it will form an imposing clump and put on a show-stopping display with its long spires of white blooms.

■ Flowers are **very attractive to butterflies** and appear at a time of year when many nectar plants have already finished flowering. Performs best in **moist soil** and will need additional water during periods of drought. ■ **FULL SUN.** ■ **ZONES 3 TO 8.**

Plant This!

Japanese anemone, *Anemone* x *hybrida*, has long been popular with gardeners looking for a colorful display in the late summer and autumn. Growing in full sun in the north and partial shade farther south, these adaptable plants bear large showy blooms on tall, wandlike stems that dance and sway in the breeze. Some varieties spread by underground runners and can become invasive. **'September Charm'** can be particularly aggressive, as can **'Elegantissima'**— especially in locations where seasonal planting of annuals or cultivation of soil for weed control disturbs their roots, causing new plants to grow abundantly. By selecting clumping rather than spreading varieties and being very careful not to disturb their shallow roots, *most* will remain welcome and well-behaved residents of the garden for many years.

Wild Swan™ Anemone

New trends in breeding have led to the development of dwarf forms, including the **Pretty Lady Series**, whose height at flowering is about half that of most varieties and has sturdy stems that remain upright, even when weighted down by autumn rains. The three current members of this series are **Pretty Lady Susan**, a single flower in rose pink; **Pretty Lady Emily**, a double flower in pale pink; and **Pretty Lady Diana**, a single flower in a deep, vibrant pink. Another recent breeding breakthrough has led to the introduction of **Wild Swan™**, a hybrid that reportedly bears white flowers from June through October, making it one of the longest-blooming anemones on the market today.

'Honorine Jobert' Anemone

One of the most popular and well-behaved of the Japanese anemones is the elegant **'Honorine Jobert'**. Pure white, poppylike blooms stand well above the foliage on sturdy 3-foot stems. Appearing from very late summer through autumn, they are one of the longest-flowering perennials in the garden and fill a difficult gap in the bloom season, especially in the South, after the summer-blooming perennials have finished and before most of the autumn-flowering perennials—asters, perennial sunflowers, goldenrods, and others—begin. The tall, sturdy stems of **'Honorine Jobert'** are perfect for cutting and the delicate-looking blooms will hold up for at least 2 to 3 days, often longer, in a vase.

■ **May suffer** in the heat and humidity of the Deep South; more shade is needed the farther south you try to grow them. Needs sufficient snow cover north of Zone 6. Avoid root disturbance to control spread. Deep, rich, moist soil. ■ **PART SUN TO PART SHADE.** ■ **ZONES 5B TO 8A.**

Plant This!

Most gardeners plant **mint** (*Mentha* species and cultivars) for its usefulness in the kitchen, whether as an herb for food recipes, an important ingredient of teas, or simply as an attractive and fragrant garnish. Be aware that nearly every culinary mint has a large and rapidly spreading system of roots and runners that allows it to expand at a mind-boggling rate when planted in the open garden. Most mints can spread 3 to 4 feet or more in a single season, and while not the most difficult of plants to extract, their rate of advance is enough to keep them well ahead of most gardeners once they're established. These members of the mint family have similar effect in the garden, but with showier flowers and noninvasive growth habit. Confine your culinary mints to pots.

'Walker's Low' Catmint

Nepeta x *faassenii* 'Walker's Low' is a member of the group of mints known as the "catmints." Readily available and easy to grow, it is a hardy, low-growing perennial with gray-green foliage and light blue flowers that are extremely attractive to a wide range of desirable pollinators in the garden. In midsummer, if plants cease flowering or begin to look worse for wear, simply cut them back hard, fertilize, and water them, and in a few weeks' time they will be back as beautiful as ever. A similar selection, **'Six Hills Giant'**, is also popular and widely grown. Larger in all respects, its deeper blue flowers make it a beautiful addition to the garden while longer stems make it nice for cutting. Though not grown for culinary purposes, the stems and foliage do have a pleasant fragrance that falls somewhere between minty and fruity.

▨ **Blooms throughout summer** and is attractive to butterflies and other beneficial pollinators. One of the few perennials that provides that elusive "blue" flower that so many gardeners long for. **Needs well-drained soil** and may suffer in heavy clay soils. ▪ **FULL SUN.** ▪ **ZONES 4 TO 8.**

Anise Hyssop

While altogether different in appearance, **Agastache rupestris** and its selected varieties are cousins of the culinary mints and are indispensable for attracting desirable pollinators—hummingbirds, butterflies, and honeybees—to the garden. Popular hybrids such as **'Apricot Sunrise'**, **'Firebird'**, and **'Tutti Frutti'** have fragrant foliage, as well as strikingly colored flowers in shades ranging from golden-orange to pink to nearly red. Native to the southwest United States, these plants are tough and adaptable, though they prefer soils that are on the dry side and not too fertile. Overfeeding and overwatering will encourage lush growth at the expense of flowers, so get them established and then *leave them alone*. They will reward you tenfold.

■ **Most hyssops are tough,** forgiving, and easily grown. Extremely attractive to butterflies. Excellent drainage is important. ■ **FULL SUN.** ■ **ZONES 5B TO 8.**

Plant This!

'Miss Manners' Obedient Plant

Flowering in mid- to late summer with attractive snapdragon-like blooms in shades of pink or white, *Physostegia virginiana*, **obedient plant** or **false dragonhead**, has long been a popular garden plant. Flowering during the long, hot days of summer, it is a welcome addition to the garden in a season when many plants, especially those in warmer climates with longer growing seasons, are not at their finest. It should be noted, however, that the name **obedient plant** does not come from its growth habit. Far from it, in fact, as it can be one of the most pernicious of garden pests if allowed to get a good foothold. Spreading by deeply rooted underground stolons, it can form enormous colonies and doesn't much care what gets in its way.

Introduced a number years ago and very similar to (perhaps the same as) the cultivar 'Alba', **'Miss Manners'** is a white-flowering form whose overall habit is less invasive than the species, as well as the vast majority of other cultivars on the market. With a more compact habit, it stands staunchly upright (correcting another bad habit of the species, which flops), flowers earlier in the season, and continues blooming well into autumn if deadheaded regularly. Many gardeners who have previous experience with obedient plant and its rampant ways may pause at the thought of planting it at all, but 'Miss Manners' is desirable, even in smaller gardens.

■ Obedient plant makes an **excellent cut flower.** 'Miss Manners' is the only variety that is garden-worthy. Most cultivars are best left to open meadows and the wildest fringes of the garden where they can behave as they will. ■ **FULL SUN.** ■ **ZONES 3 TO 9.**

Blue Vervain

Even if 'Miss Manners' gives you cause for pause, consider growing the beautiful native **blue vervain**, *Verbena hastata*, an often overlooked but delightful and well-behaved verbena with flowers that are smaller than, but in some ways similar to, obedient plant. Flowering from July to September with densely packed spikes of small, violet-blue flowers, it also makes an excellent cut flower. Growing wild across the prairies of the central United States, blue vervain is a tough, adaptable perennial whose noninvasive habit makes it perfect for gardens of all sizes.

■ **Well-behaved native** alternative to the more aggressive obedient plant. **Very attractive to butterflies and many beneficial pollinators,** drawing them into the garden from some distance away. Long stems and long vase life make it an excellent choice for a cut flower in informal arrangements. ■ **FULL SUN.** ■ **ZONES 4 TO 8.**

OSTRICH FERN

Plant This!

It may be difficult to think of a fern as being invasive, but in the context of the garden, there are several that are aggressive enough to be problematic if not given ample elbow room. One of those is the **ostrich fern**, *Matteucia struthiopteris*, whose groundcovering habit may be welcome in the open woodland but is less desirable in garden beds and borders. Spreading by underground stolons, offspring may pop up as far as 4 feet away from the mother plant, quickly working their way across a large expanse. Similar experiences may be had with the **New York fern**, *Thelypteris noveboracensis*, in the North and with the **southern wood fern**, *Thelypteris kunthii*, in the South, both of which will creep and form large colonies over time.

Cinnamon Fern

If it's the "classic" fern appearance you love and wish to add to your garden, **cinnamon fern**, *Osmunda cinnamomea*, tops the list. Perhaps no other fern is so beautiful in the spring when the large, silver-haired fiddleheads emerge and unfurl to reveal apple green fronds reaching up to 3 feet tall. Old, established clumps will form a large, mounded, woody rootstock from which the fronds emerge in early spring and these should be left undisturbed, as the plants will only become more impressive with age. Cinnamon fern bears two sets of fronds each season: one fertile and almost shriveled in appearance, where new spores are borne in early spring, and the other sterile, which are the broad, leafy fronds that we associate with this fern's great beauty. One of the most heat-tolerant ferns, it will perform well as far south as Zone 7 and occasionally in even warmer regions, given a shady location and deep, rich, moist soil. Cinnamon fern will thrive as far north as Zones 3 and prefers part sun to shade.

Christmas Fern

Christmas fern, *Polystichum acrostichoides*, is an outstanding and durable garden plant with an exceptionally broad range. Hardy from Zones 4 to 8, it thrives in a wide range of locations, from bright, open woodlands to fairly deep shade. While its leaves are not as finely divided as some, it retains that classic fern form that so many gardeners desire and has the added benefit of being partly (farther north) to fully (farther south) evergreen. A strict clump-former, it is never invasive, and while occasional sporelings may pop up around the garden, they are rarely unwelcome and are easily transplanted if they appear in less-than-ideal locations. Because it is so good natured, it combines easily with hostas, hellebores, and woodland wildflowers, always friendly and never a thug.

■ Ferns come in a **vast array of forms** from around the world. Some are sun lovers, while others grow in deep shade. **Much is written** about ferns and with minimal research, selection of an appropriate variety for any garden should be relatively simple. ■ **SUN TO SHADE.** ■ **ZONES 2 TO 10,** depending on species.

PINK EVENING PRIMROSE

Plant This!

Attracted by pots full of showy pink flowers at nurseries and garden centers, we excitedly plant this beautiful and delicate-looking wildflower only to discover the following season that it has taken over most, if not all, of the perennial garden or border and has invaded every desirable specimen along the way. Once established, little can be done to curb the spread of **pink evening primrose** (*Oenothera speciosa*). Left to its own devices, it will stretch from one end of the garden to the other in a single season, maybe two. Still, for some reason, it remains widely grown and quite popular among gardeners. Its nearly indestructible nature does make it useful in exceptionally difficult locations—street curbs, hell strips, neglected mailboxes, and the like—but it has no place in the cultivated garden.

Yellow Sundrops

While most other species of *Oenothera* sport yellow flowers instead of the soft pink that seems to delight everyone so much with *Oenothera speciosa* (with some exceptions), there are a number of selections that make more than worthy garden additions and *Oenothera fruticosa*, **yellow sundrops**, tops that list. Represented by cultivars such as **'Fireworks'** and **'Sonnenwende'** (**'Summer Solstice'**), these politely spreading but noninvasive varieties brighten the early to midsummer garden with golden yellow blooms that shimmer in the morning light. **'Fireworks'** is particularly attractive, with bright red stems and buds that open to yellow flowers. **'Cold Crick'** is a dwarf form growing only 8 to 12 inches tall, but with exceptional flower power.

'Shimmer' Evening Primrose

A newer introduction, *Oenothera fremontii* 'Shimmer' has brightened my garden for the past several seasons. A low-growing, almost flat groundcover, its extremely narrow leaves of shimmering silver are the perfect complement to the soft yellow flowers that appear over an extended period from early to midsummer. Its stems will creep across the ground, but its roots stay put, making it an excellent choice for the front edges of beds and borders or a perfect selection for the rock garden. It requires full sun and good drainage and is hardy in Zones 4 through 8.

■ Most species are **tough, drought tolerant, and showy** in bloom. Evening primroses are truly low-maintenance plants that simply want to be left alone, once established. Silver-leafed forms offer attractive foliage in addition to showy flowers. Well-drained soil. ■ **FULL SUN.** ■ **ZONES 4 TO 8.**

Plant This!

Globe Bellflower

The **globe bellflower**, *Campanula glomerata*, is a well-behaved, clumping species that is adaptable to a wider range of climates than many others. More heat tolerant, it will even make its home in the South, providing early to midsummer blooms in deep shades of violet-blue. **'Joan Elliott'** and **'Superba'** are particularly nice forms, the latter having the best heat tolerance of the group.

Bellflowers have long been popular due to their prominence in so many English gardening books and magazines. Lured by their unique, bell-shaped blooms, frequently in the most lustful shade of blue, American gardeners are tempted to try their own hand at growing them successfully. Unfortunately, not all bellflowers are created equal (and not all of them are blue!), and some species—*Campanula punctata*, the **spotted bellflower**, and its hybrids in particular—can be aggressive groundcovers that will invade nearby plants. When it comes time to move or divide those plants, the bellflower tags along, and soon you have it spreading all over the garden. The cultivars **'Mulberry Rose'**, **'Cherry Bells'**, and **'Pink Octopus'**, all selections or hybrids of the spotted bellflower, have all proven at least somewhat aggressive.

■ Most species are **best suited to cooler climates,** but some will thrive farther south. Under ideal conditions, even some newer cultivars may be aggressive. Watch for possible thugs. Many are **good choices for rock gardens** with excellent drainage. ■ **FULL TO PART SUN.** ■ **ZONES 3 TO 8,** depending on species.

Carpathian Harebell

The most widely known and popular of the bellflowers is the **Carpathian harebell**, *Campanula carpatica*. Best suited to cooler climates, it is the epitome of what a bellflower should be with its bright, sky blue flowers completely hiding the foliage when it is in full bloom in early summer. It is perfect for bed and border edges or as a rock garden plant. It spreads slowly and may reseed. **'Blue Clips'** and **'White Clips'** are readily available and excellent performers with some of the largest flowers of any selections.

'Purple Robe' Nierembergia

For a similar look, but with built-in heat and drought tolerance, try the annual **cupflower**, *Nierembergia* 'Purple Robe'. In hot summer climates where many bellflowers struggle, cupflower will fill their place with the greatest of ease. With cup-shaped, blue to light purple blooms, it gives a comparable effect to the shorter bellflowers in the garden, flowering throughout the summer with a modicum of care.

Plant This!

Lured by the stunning color of its silvery white, finely divided leaves, many gardeners plant **white sage**, *Artemisia ludoviciana*, not knowing that it likely ranks in the top ten garden aggressors and will quickly take over entire beds with its invasive roots. Once established, it is nearly impossible to control. **'Silver King'** and **'Silver Queen'** are the two most commonly offered varieties; they are similar in size, but 'Silver Queen' has wider and more deeply cut leaves. Both are equally aggressive. A less invasive form, **'Valerie Finnis'**, has become popular but seems intolerant of regions where summer heat and humidity prevail. The plant looks ratty by midsummer and rarely recovers to a satisfactory appearance, even when the weather cools in autumn.

■ **'Powis Castle'** and **'Huntington'** artemisia are woody perennials with a shrublike growth habit. Pruning should occur in early to mid-spring; no winter pruning. A light trimming in midsummer will encourage new growth to sprout, keeping plants tidy until season's end. Well-drained soil. ■ **FULL SUN.** ■ **ZONES 4 TO 8.**

'Powis Castle' Artemisia

For gardeners across most of the United States, **Artemisia x 'Powis Castle'** should be the wormwood, or artemisia, of choice. North of Zone 6, it can be grown as a fast-growing and useful annual, while farther south it is a reliable and indispensable perennial, almost shrublike in its habit. Its finely filigreed leaves offer silvery white color in a plant that is both refined and reliable. It is the finest artemisia for southern gardens, tolerating heat and humidity as well as damp winters, where other members of the genus would soon suffer from and probably succumb to a variety of fungal diseases. Closely related and similar in appearance is *Artemisia* x **'Huntington'**, with equally silver foliage that is soft to the touch and, to some noses, pleasantly fragrant when brushed past in the garden. Its heat and humidity tolerance appears to equal that of **'Powis Castle'**. Both selections are outstanding subjects as fillers for pots, thriving in full sun and with the excellent drainage that growing in a container provides.

Dusty Miller

An annual in most climates, but an excellent heat- and humidity-tolerant substitute for the fussier or invasive species of *Artemisia*, **dusty miller**, *Jacobaea maritima*, is a workhorse in the garden. Its silvery gray leaves may be deeply notched and lobed, or so finely divided as to have a fernlike texture, depending on the variety. Drought tolerant once established, it can be used as an informal filler in perennial beds and borders but was also prized by the Victorians for use in their formal and colorful bedding schemes.

CHAPTER 2

Perennials— Improved Species

G ardeners are often overwhelmed when strolling through their local garden centers by the sheer number of new plant varieties that hit the market each spring. How do you know which one is the best one for your garden? While there are no cut-and-dried answers, the best place to begin is by asking questions of garden center staff or gardening friends who may also be experimenting with new varieties, maybe doing a little Internet research, or by consulting a book like this one.

The ability to produce tens or even hundreds of thousands of plants in a very short period of time—a process known as "tissue culture"—has changed the way plants enter the market today. When a new plant is discovered with a better growth habit, a variegated leaf, or a new flower color, that plant can be on the market within a year's time, perhaps two, at the most. Unfortunately, that has led to many plants being introduced before they are tested and proven to grow well in the garden, which in turn has led to many disappointed and frustrated gardeners whose plants did not perform up to their expectations.

In the following pages, we'll try to take some of the guesswork out which

of the new varieties might be worthy additions to your own garden, especially where some of today's most popular garden plants such as purple coneflower and Lenten rose are concerned. Coralbells are another group where it seems like hundreds of new varieties (though it's really fewer than that) are seen on garden center shelves each spring. How do you know which plants will be hardy in your gardening zone, and will they be both winter hardy, with the ability to tolerate freezing temperatures, but also summer hardy and able to stand the onslaught of heat and humidity experienced in some regions? Read on to find the answers for those questions and more.

INSTEAD OF
OLD-FASHIONED BEARDED IRIS

Plant This!

Tough, resilient, indestructible—those may be a few words that come to mind when gardeners think of **bearded iris** (*Iris* hybrids). All three words are true. Popular for hundreds of years and grown in temperate climates around the world, the bearded iris may be spread further across the globe than almost any other group of hardy garden plants. Available in a virtual rainbow of colors, from pure white to inky black, from golden yellows to the deepest purples and even the elusive blue, bearded iris are classic and timeless in the way few other flowers are except, perhaps, the rose. Thriving with only a modicum of care, bearded irises are at their finest when the interaction from gardeners is at its least—the ultimate low-maintenance garden plant!

'Flying Solo' Bearded Iris

At the opposite end of the spectrum are some of today's newest and most modern hybrids, among them the outstanding **'Flying Solo'**. A leader in the pack of today's median (mid-sized) bearded iris, this little plant has it all—scrumptious color, excellent substance, disease resistance, and flower power! Mature clumps have been known to have more than forty blooms open at once, making it a standout in any garden. A wide range of median bearded irises is now on the market, with new and improved varieties being introduced each year. **'Garnet Slippers'**, in the most sumptuous shade of deep, garnet red, is another of the median group that deserves to be more widely grown.

52

'Swerti' Bearded Iris

Steeped in history, some of the earliest hybrid flowers grown in gardens were bearded iris. **'Swerti'**, a naturally occurring hybrid dating back to 1612, is one such plant. Celebrating its 400th birthday in 2012, it is still grown by collectors today and, due to its unique habit of bearing unusually small blooms in unusually large quantity, is seemingly poised for a well-deserved resurgence in popularity.

'Well Endowed' Bearded Iris

If you like your bearded iris big, they don't come much bigger than **'Well Endowed'**. Almost indescribably bright, its enormous golden yellow flowers borne atop 36-inch stems are brilliant beacons in the garden. Perfectly paired with the blue-flowering clematis **'H. F. Young'**, the two combine to put on a spectacular spring show that lasts nearly a month.

▨ Available in a rainbow of colors, iris make **outstanding cut flowers** for late spring, early summer. Easy, adaptable, and tolerant of poor soil. **Iris despise being too wet,** especially in summer when they are dormant. Useful in stabilizing slopes. ▨ **FULL TO PART SUN.** ▨ **ZONES 3 TO 10.**

OLD-FASHIONED CORALBELLS

Coralbells (*Heuchera* species and hybrids) have long been popular for their tidy mounds of semievergreen foliage and long, wiry wands of red flowers that appear from spring through early summer. For many years, breeding coralbells was centered in Europe, using European species that were less well suited to growing in many American gardens. A lack of heat tolerance made them feasible only for gardeners in the northern tier of states and the Pacific Northwest, as plants typically melted in the heat and humidity of summers below the Mason-Dixon line. A renaissance began in the 1990s when several enterprising plant breeders began working with species native to the United States, making breakthroughs not only in leaf color and pattern, but also in heat and humidity tolerance. Today, *Heuchera* and their kin are some of the most popular shade garden plants in America.

Plant This!

'Caramel' Coralbells

By using the southeastern native species *Heuchera villosa*, hybridizers have been able to impart heat and humidity tolerance to a broad range of varieties now available to gardeners everywhere. One of the best is **'Caramel'**, with unusual toffee-colored leaves. Its vigor and ability to thrive in dry shade have made it one of the most popular introductions of the past decade. Following close on its heels are varieties such as **'Southern Comfort'**, **'Merlot'**, and **'Autumn Bride'**, which have helped to expand the color palette with leaves ranging from chartreuse to burgundy.

■ **Colorful foliage** throughout the year makes coralbells indispensible in the shade garden. Plants with fuzzy leaves indicate hybrids with *Heuchera americana* or *Heuchera villosa*, **native species** well suited to Southern gardens. Some varieties also have showy flowers excellent for cutting. ■ **PART SHADE TO SHADE.** ■ **ZONES 4 TO 8.**

'Sugar Plum' Coralbells

If it's a bright spot you need in a shady corner, try one of the coralbell varieties with silver-patterned leaves. **'Sugar Plum'** has leaves in a rich shade of burgundy heavily overlaid with shining pewter, while varieties such as **'Blackberry Currant'** offer plum-purple leaves patterned in silver. Flowers are generally small and white to greenish-white on these varieties, which are grown primarily for their foliage.

Heucherella, a *Heuchera* x *Tiarella* Hybrid

The introduction of hybrids between *Heuchera* and their close relatives *Tiarella* (foamflower), known as *Heucherella*, continues to expand the range of leaf forms, colors, and growth habits. Foamflower has lent its maple-shaped leaves to the ever-growing number of hybrids, and the spreading form of the species has opened many new doors to hybridizers. Trailing and spreading varieties are now popular as groundcovers and for fillers in pots and hanging baskets.

INSTEAD OF
OLD-FASHIONED BEDDING DAHLIA

Plant This!

For many years, gardeners had two choices when it came to **dahlias** (*Dahlia* hybrids): the dwarf bedding types that grow into squatty, graceless plants with oversized blooms that don't match the plants' stature, or bags full of bareroot tubers that produce the high-maintenance, cutting-type dahlias with flowers ranging in size from a ping pong ball to a dinner plate and that demand attention to attain peak performance. The dwarf types despise heat and humidity, looking like sad, green lumps for much of the summer until cooler fall weather arrives. The cutting types require copious amounts of fertilizer and water, precise staking, pinching, disbudding, and constant care to produce the finest flowers. For these reasons and more, dahlias fell out of favor with many gardeners.

Mystic Dahlia Series

Recently, Dr. Keith Hammett of Auckland, New Zealand, has made great advances in breeding modern dahlias with distinctive foliage and flowers with the ability to bloom nonstop throughout the summer, despite heat and humidity. Dahlias in the **Mystic Series** sport deep burgundy to nearly black leaves that are deeply cut and very attractive, forming the perfect backdrop for showy, single flowers in clean, bright colors held aloft on long stems that are perfect for cutting. Included in the series are 'Mystic Illusion,' with sunflower yellow blooms and a dark center against nearly black leaves, and 'Mystic Enchantment,' whose blooms open vivid scarlet and fade to a warm, burnt orange against burgundy foliage. 'Mystic Wonder' (velvety red blooms), 'Mystic Dreamer' (soft pink and white-striped blooms), 'Mystic Haze' (apricot-orange kissed with gold), 'Mystic Spirit' (peachy-apricot), 'Mystic Fantasy' (flamingo pink with a soft yellow halo), and 'Mystic Memories' (soft peach, blushed red) currently round out the series, with future introductions being planned.

The Mystic Series of dahlias have been bred for strong, sturdy stems that do not require staking, and because their line of breeding includes species native to hotter and drier climates, they are much more forgiving of tougher garden conditions than their old-fashioned counterparts. Plants are easy to grow, vigorous, and produce hundreds of flowers per plant during the growing season. While regular deadheading is helpful to keep plants flowering profusely, these dahlias are extremely pest and disease resistant, and little other maintenance is required.

■ **Outstanding cut flower** with long stems and attractive foliage. Dahlias are **heavy feeders and need regular watering** to promote heavy bloom. Tubers may be dug and stored for winter in dry peat or sawdust in colder zones. ■ **FULL SUN.** ■ **ANNUAL IN ZONES 3 TO 6; PERENNIAL IN ZONES 7 TO 9.**

OLD-FASHIONED DAYLILY

Plant This!

Daylilies (*Hemerocallis* species and hybrids) have been enjoyed in gardens for thousands of years with historical references being made to them in China since before the time of Confucius (551–479 BC). Serious hybridizing began in the late 1800s when the first registered cross, 'Apricot', was introduced in 1893 and given the Award of Merit by the Royal Horticultural Society the same year. Since then, professional plant breeders and backyard hobbyists have registered nearly 75,000 hybrids through the American Hemerocallis Society, and their popularity shows no signs of waning. With the introduction of the first tetraploid daylilies in 1947, the daylily world changed forever. Larger blooms, sturdier stems, more robust growth, and a virtual rainbow of colors were but a few of the traits soon to appear on the horizon.

'Forsyth Comanche' Daylily

The ability to rebloom multiple times during the season is a long sought-after trait in daylilies. With the introduction of 'Stella d'Oro' in the late 1970s, repeat flowering has been at the top of most hybridizers' lists of desirable features in new daylily introductions. Until recently, this reblooming trait was most common in what might be called "landscape daylilies," but modern hybrids such as 'Forsyth Comanche' and many others have the ability to rebloom too. This breakthrough means that daylilies that once had a rigidly set window of time when they flowered now have the ability to produce new blooms periodically throughout the growing season, sometimes turning a few weeks of bloom into several months.

■ **Tough, durable, and easy-to-grow.** There are three types: those with dormant, semievergreen, or evergreen foliage. In Zone 5 and colder, dormant or semidormant varieties are the most winter hardy. ■ **FULL TO PART SUN.** ■ **ZONES 3 TO 9,** depending on variety.

'Nosferatu' Daylily

Further advancements in breeding have flattened the flowers; widened the petals; increased the thickness of the petals, making them more durable against wind and rain; and improved the color range to include nearly every color of the rainbow except true blue. 'Nosferatu', with its deep, rich color; wide petals; and ability to withstand fading in the sun has made it exceptionally popular since its introduction in 1990. Today's hybridizers continue to expand the color range, the color patterns, and the flower forms, including spider types with individual petals up to 7 inches long, double forms with so many petals the flowers look almost like cupcakes, and crested forms with unique and interesting ridges and "feathers" on the petals.

Daylilies with a lighter background color and darker "eyes" have been popular since their initial introduction. Modern breeding has expanded this concept into lighter watermarks and halos and, most recently, broken color patterns that are kaleidoscopic in nature, offering nearly endless possible color combinations within a single flower, while intricate petal edges with large ruffles, often in complementary colors to the body of the flower, continue to push the boundaries of every hybridizer's dreams.

'Tetrina's Daughter' Daylily

Early tetraploid hybrids (those having double the normal number of chromosomes in their DNA) were nothing like today's modern hybrids. Plants such as **'Tetrina's Daughter'** maintained their open and somewhat spidery form, but acted as important bridge plants between the earliest hybrids and today's modern flowers. Because of their outstanding garden performance, they remain popular even now.

OLD-FASHIONED GARDEN PHLOX

Garden phlox, *Phlox paniculata*, has enjoyed immense popularity in perennial gardens for more than 100 years. Native to the eastern and southeastern United States, it is perfectly suited to American gardens, but it has made its way to Europe and other parts of the world as well. Where it grows wild, it is a tough, adaptable, and durable plant, but when it is given the royal treatment—good soil, a wealth of nutrients, and regular (often overhead) irrigation—in a garden setting, it becomes susceptible to a variety of frustrating and often unattractive problems. If you were to play a word association game with most gardeners, the words most commonly associated with garden phlox would be "powdery mildew." Fortunately, modern selections have been chosen for their disease resistance and durability.

Plant This!

'David' Garden Phlox

'David' was the first of the truly disease-resistant garden phlox to be introduced to the market more than twenty years ago. Its pure white, fragrant flowers and ability to resist the onslaught of powdery mildew even at the height of summer's heat and humidity have earned it well-deserved respect from gardeners the world over. This, combined with its sturdy, upright habit and long season of bloom, earned it the Perennial Plant of the Year honor in 2002.

■ **Fragrant blooms** make perfect and long-lasting cut flowers. **Extremely attractive to butterflies and desirable pollinators.** One of the biggest contributors to powdery mildew on garden phlox is overhead irrigation. Good air circulation and keeping leaves dry helps prevent mildew. ■ **FULL TO PART SUN.** ■ **ZONES 4 TO 8.**

'Jeana' Garden Phlox

A plant that has been floating around for several years amongst collectors and gardeners in the know is *Phlox paniculata* **'Jeana'**. Discovered by plantswoman Jeana Prewitt in a rural area a few miles outside of Nashville, Tennessee, this charming and unique garden phlox deserves much wider recognition. Remaining completely powdery mildew-free, even in the hottest and most humid of summers, **'Jeana'** bears small, but sweetly scented flowers in varying shades of lavender-pink from midsummer through autumn. Due to its almost complete sterility, it sets little to no seed, putting all of its energy back into flowering, which it does for months on end.

'Nicky' Garden Phlox

New selections soon followed in the footsteps of 'David' and one of the most brilliantly colored was **'Nicky'**, showing off in an almost alarming shade of fuchsia-purple at the height of summer. Only slightly less disease resistant than 'David', 'Nicky' may occasionally suffer mild outbreaks of powdery mildew, especially if water is being applied overhead, but rarely to the extent that it becomes problematic as it does on so many garden phlox.

INSTEAD OF
'GOLDSTURM' BLACK-EYED SUSAN

Plant This!

When it comes to mid- and late summer flowering perennials, few other plants command attention like the **black-eyed Susans**, especially 'Goldsturm' (*Rudbeckia fulgida* 'Goldsturm'). The common name applies to a number of plants, all closely related and most bearing a daisylike bloom in some shade of yellow to gold, occasionally marked in red or rust, with a dramatically dark and contrasting central cone of black or brown. Most are unfussy and easy to grow, making them some of the first perennials that many new gardeners try their hand at growing. Fortunately, their efforts are usually met with a fair degree of success, and with a newfound burst of confidence they are encouraged to try their hands at growing other plants.

■ Rudbeckias are among the **easiest and most forgiving perennials** to grow. Overfertilizing can lead to their flowering stems being weak and not standing upright. Good winter drainage is essential. Excellent cut flowers and very attractive to butterflies and other pollinators. ■ **FULL TO PART SUN.** ■ **ZONES 4 TO 8.**

'Little Henry' Black-Eyed Susan

Perhaps the most highly praised and beautifully flowered of recent black-eyed Susan introductions has been *Rudbeckia subtomentosa* **'Henry Eilers'** with its unique wheel-like blooms given their dramatic effect by the fact that their petals, instead of being flat, are tubular or quilled. Flowering in a bright, but pleasing shade of medium yellow, they aren't as garish as some of their deep gold- or orange-flowered kin, and the flower's form refines it even further. Henry's only inherent problem is that he grows rather tall—nearly 6 feet under good conditions—and his stems are somewhat weak, so he tends to spill over his neighbors. Enter **'Little Henry'**, whose overall height is one-third shorter, maturing at 4 feet and whose strong stems hold its blooms more upright. Flowers are nearly identical to 'Henry Eilers' and appear from midsummer until frost with little or no deadheading required.

Numerous other species exist. Most are extremely attractive to pollinators, which every garden needs more of, and goldfinches and other small birds will cover the plants in late summer and autumn to strip them over their seed.

Rudbeckia speciosa var. *newmanii*

A closely related species to 'Goldsturm', *Rudbeckia speciosa* var. *newmanii* is an often overlooked perennial black-eyed Susan whose leaves are coarsely toothed and serrated, making the foliage more attractive than its popular cousin and giving it textural appeal in addition to its beautiful blooms. This plant has a wildflowery appearance about it, as though it just came from the meadow. Its deep orange flowers are nearly 3 inches across and are carried on strong, straight stems reaching 24 to 30 inches tall, making them perfect for cutting. Not as common in garden centers, it is worth searching out online from some of the better mail-order nurseries.

Hostas (*Hosta* species and hybrids like daylilies), are represented by literally thousands of varieties, each with a slight variation in color, leaf pattern, shape, or size. Ubiquitous, yet indispensible, they thrive in the shady spots along garden paths in nearly every region of the country except those that don't experience the cold winter dormancy hostas need in order to thrive. From Zone 8 northward to Zone 3, hostas frequently form the backbone of the summer shade garden, spreading their broad leaves regally amongst finer leaved ferns, astilbes, bleeding hearts, and an array of ephemeral spring wildflowers. Continued breeding efforts and the selection of naturally occurring mutations called "sports" keep the hosta fresh and new, with countless offerings being added each year to the already enormous list of choices.

Plant This!

'Dragon Tails' Hosta

From tiny, groundcovering plants such as **'Dragon Tails'**, reaching only 4 inches tall and spreading politely around the feet of other shade garden plants, to the gargantuan **'Empress Wu'**, the world's largest hosta measuring in at a whopping 4 feet tall by 6 feet wide, hostas rule the shade garden in temperate climates. Today's hybridizers and gardeners are looking for plants with thick, heavy leaves—what they call "substance" in the hosta world—that are resistant to slug and snail damage. The best ones are almost rubbery or leathery in texture. New color combinations and variegation patterns are also highly sought, as are fragrant flowers and heat tolerance.

■ Entire books are devoted to the subject of hostas and their seemingly **endless varieties.** Size may range from plants just a few inches tall and wide to those that will reach upwards of 4 feet tall by 6 feet across. Rich, moist soil. ■ **PART SUN TO FULL SHADE.** ■ **ZONES 3 TO 8.**

'Liberty' Hosta

Bold variegation in patterns of gold, chartreuse, and white brighten shady nooks. 'Liberty'—with its upright vase shape, large size, and dramatic variegation—is one of the finest choices for gardens in both the North and South. Used singly as a striking focal point or in large masses as deciduous groundcover, it always stops garden visitors in their tracks. When well grown, there are few other hostas that can achieve its level of style and beauty.

'Paradise Glory' Hosta

Variegated in reverse with the brighter color appearing in the center of each leaf, **'Paradise Glory'** is a newer and more dramatic version of the classic hosta **'Paul's Glory'**. Very thick blue-green leaves are highlighted by a bold central flare of golden yellow and pale lavender, and slightly fragrant flowers appear on tall stems in midsummer. Its size makes it even more dramatic, with its 24-inch height by 40-inch spread making it one of the larger hostas in the garden, showing off its coloration to great effect.

65

Plant This!

Lenten rose, *Helleborus* species and hybrids, and its relatives are perfect examples of a group of plants in this book that, instead of recommending a replacement species for one that is less desirable, focuses on new and improved varieties and modern advancements in the breeding and distribution of plants already loved by gardeners. Over the past three decades, the **Lenten roses** and their kin have been completely transformed by diligent hybridizers, from an unusual perennial dwelling in the shady corners of collectors' gardens to an indispensable shade garden staple. A plant whose nodding, bell-shaped flowers were solid green or heavily suffused with green now holds its flowers proudly aloft, facing its viewers in clear, pure colors and in forms that fewer than two decades ago gardeners only dreamed of.

Golden Lotus™ Lenten Rose

Perhaps the greatest achievement in the creation of new **hybrid hellebores** is the realization of fully double flowers like those of the **Golden Lotus™** strain, each containing a number of petals well beyond the typical five. While double-flowered plants have existed for some time, it was only with the advent of tissue culture and the ability to produce those plants quickly and in large numbers that they became widely available to the home gardener.

■ Most hybrid Lenten rose take **three years** in the garden **to become fully established** and begin performing to their greatest potential. Excellent for cutting and arranging in winter. Rich, well-draining soil. ■ **PART SHADE TO SHADE.** ■ **ZONES 5** (with protection) **TO 8.**

Golden Sunrise™ Lenten Rose

Among the most sought after of colors in Lenten rose by both hybridizers and gardeners alike is a pure, clear yellow. While that goal has yet to be truly achieved, each new generation of hybrids brings more saturated yellow flowers to the market, some with striking red eye zones and others with dark speckling or "brushstrokes" on their petals. The day is close at hand when a pure, buttery yellow that holds its color for a long period of time will be achieved. The **Golden Sunrise™** strain from the breeding program of Ernie and Marietta O'Byrne of Northwest Garden Nursery takes a giant leap in that direction, their golden yellow flowers appearing in late winter and early spring in gardens from Zone 5 to Zone 8b.

'Tutu' Lenten Rose

Equally as popular as the doubles are those known as the **anemone-flowered** forms, their blooms having a well-developed ruff of petaloid nectaries at the center of the bloom, not unlike a Victorian lace collar. The fascinating intricacies of the flowers on varieties such as **'Tutu'** make for endless discussions among gardening friends and months of beauty in the garden.

OLD-FASHIONED LILY

Plant This!

'Conca d'Or' Orienpet Lily

One of the greatest breakthroughs in lily breeding in the twentieth century occurred when the **trumpet lilies**, with their long, fluted blooms and exciting range of colors, met the wide open, fragrant flowers of the **oriental lilies**. These marriages made in horticultural heaven created what are now known as the **Orienpet hybrid lilies**. Combining the best attributes of both groups, these hybrids opened the flowers of the trumpet lilies to show their beautiful faces and broadened the color palette of the oriental lilies into shades never before seen. One of the first, **'Conca d'Or'**, rises to heights of more than 6 feet under ideal conditions and has been known to produce more than 200 golden yellow flowers in a single season from a mature and well-established clump.

Appearing in the garden from early summer to early autumn, depending on the species or cultivar, **lilies** (*Lilium* species and hybrids) seem to impart a sense that the gardener who lives and works here knows what they're doing. They bring a refined elegance to even the wildest of gardens or natural areas, and most are tougher and more forgiving than one might think of so beautiful a flower. While there is certainly nothing wrong with the old-fashioned cultivars— many of them are still extremely popular—there is, or should be, room in almost every garden for experimenting with some of the newer and more modern hybrids. These combine the very best characteristics of the beloved classics with never-before-seen color combinations, vigor, and resistance to pests and disease.

'Silk Road' Orienpet Lily

'Silk Road' also combines the best of both worlds: the height and sturdy stems of the trumpet lilies with the color and fragrance of the oriental hybrids. Putting on a tremendous display in mid- to late summer, it opens its rich pink flowers edged in white for nearly a month as its heady fragrance drifts across the garden with a warm summer breeze.

'Touch' Orienpet Lily

Perhaps the greatest surprises of all to come from the crossing of the trumpet and oriental lilies were the astounding color combinations that appeared in their offspring. Golden yellows and soft oranges with deep red throats and brushstrokes up the petals were the stuff dreams were made of and those dreams had become reality. Varieties such as **'Touch'** set new standards for what the lily could be and the direction for where the next generation might go.

■ **Lilies require rich, deep, well-drained soil** to reach their maximum potential in the garden. Plant in groups of three to five or more bulbs in large, well-prepared holes thoroughly amended with compost. May take two to three seasons to reach maturity. ■ **FULL TO PART SUN**. ■ **ZONES 4 TO 8.**

LUNGWORT

Plant This!

Lungwort (*Pulmonaria* species and hybrids) is another perfect example of an old-fashioned garden plant that, because of new and improved selections, has seen a recent resurgence in popularity. The addition of **long-leafed lungwort**, *Pulmonaria longifolia*, to many hybridizers' breeding programs has doubled the size of the plants, making them all the showier, and increased their resistance to foliar diseases such as powdery mildew, which ruined many of the old selections by midsummer. Flowers appear in early spring before the plants' primary flush of foliage, often opening pink and turning blue before falling, making them excellent companions for many of native spring ephemerals such as bloodroot, golden ragwort, and celandine poppy.

'Raspberry Splash' Lungwort

Equally as impressive in gardens everywhere is **'Raspberry Splash'**. Also showing its long-leafed lungwort heritage, the very long, deep green leaves are dramatically spotted in silver, providing the perfect backdrop for the sensational clusters of raspberry-purple flowers in early spring. Mixed with early-flowering golden yellow daffodils, the color combination is eye-catching and cheerful, if a little gauche, but who among us isn't ready for a little gauche after a long, gray winter? A lesser known and naturally occurring variety **'Cevennensis'**, from the Cevennes in France, may well be the most dramatic of all with individual leaves, spotted and speckled in silver, measuring up to 2 feet long, forming clumps nearly 4 feet wide! A show-stopper, surely, when well grown.

■ Lungworts require **rich, humus-laden, and consistently moist soil** to reach their fullest potential. Summertime drought will cause browning of the leaves, which plants will likely not recover from until the following spring when new growth emerges. Plants need good winter drainage. ■ **PART SUN TO SHADE.** ■ **ZONES 3 TO 8.**

'Trevi Fountain' Lungwort

The influence of the long-leafed lungwort in its offspring is evidenced by the exceptionally long leaves—nearly double that of old cultivars—the vigor with which they grow, and their superior resistance to powdery mildew, which plagues so many of the old varieties. Topping the list of recent introductions is **'Trevi Fountain'**, which is a stellar performer in the heat and humidity of the South, but just as much at home up north. With rich, moist soil, regular feeding, and good winter drainage, clumps may reach 30 inches in diameter at maturity, appearing, from a distance, more like an unusual, narrow-leafed hosta than a lungwort until closer inspection reveals its hairy and spotted leaves.

MAY NIGHT SALVIA

One of the earlier plants to win the Perennial Plant Association's Perennial Plant of the Year designation, *Salvia* **x** *sylvestris* **'May Night'** has been a popular garden perennial for more than twenty years. Its deep indigo flowers are borne in large, showy spires, and when grown in full sun and well-drained soil in climates with cool nights, it can be dazzling in the garden. In warmer climates, however, the blooms fade quickly, and while the plant does have the ability to rebloom several times throughout the summer, the secondary cycles are never equal to its initial display. In the right climate, the plant is certainly worth growing, but where it is less successful, gardeners have plenty of other choices in the salvia clan from which to choose.

Plant This!

'Black and Blue' Anise-Scented Sage

Not mentioning *Salvia guaranitica* 'Black and Blue' would be remiss. Wildly popular and familiar to most gardeners by now, it sets a standard for ease of growth and profusion of bloom. Flowering in that elusive shade of cobalt blue that so many gardeners desire, it is one of the finest plants for attracting hummingbirds to the garden. It is not as drought tolerant as some and performs best in richer soil with adequate moisture.

■ Sages hail from a **wide variety of climates** around the world. Some are hardy perennials while others are tender tropicals. **One of the finest groups of plants for attracting** hummingbirds and other desirable **pollinators** to your garden. ■ **FULL TO PART SUN.** ■ **ZONES 3 TO 10,** depending on species and cultivar.

'Hot Lips' Desert Sage

If heat, humidity, and drought tolerance is what you need, several salvia species from Texas and the Southwestern United States may fit the bill. *Salvia microphylla* 'Hot Lips' belongs to this group of plants that, once established, can withstand just about any weather that summer can dish out. In addition to **'Hot Lips'**, other similar choices such as **'Furman's Red'**, **'Cherry Queen'**, and **'Marashino'** continue to be popular with gardeners, attracting hummingbirds in droves to the summertime garden. With excellent winter drainage, many of these will be hardy in Zone 6 and warmer.

'Wendy's Wish' Hybrid Sage

A recently introduced hybrid, **'Wendy's Wish'** has all of the attributes every great salvia should have: deep green, glossy foliage that is unblemished by pest or disease; a tidy habit with strong stems that hold its flowers upright; and flowers in the most stunning shade of magenta pink. Add to that the fact that it blooms all summer long, regardless of day length, heat, or humidity—actually thriving in the latter—and you have one superb garden plant. If there is any drawback, it's that **'Wendy's Wish'** is an annual in all but the warmest climates. Don't let that stop you, though!

INSTEAD OF
MOONBEAM COREOPSIS

Moonbeam coreopsis, *Coreopsis verticillata* 'Moonbeam', has long been among gardeners' favorites for its finely textured foliage, soft yellow flowers, exceptionally long bloom season, and ease of growth. It performs well in a wide range of zones; is tolerant of clay soils, heat, and humidity; and is resistant to most pests and diseases, though powdery mildew can be a problem in the heat and humidity of the Southeast. While its many positive attributes have bolstered its popularity for more than two decades, recent advances in breeding have led to a range of plants that offer more in the way of disease resistance, length of flowering season, and a greatly expanded color range beyond shades of yellow and gold.

Plant This!

BIG BANG™ 'Mercury Rising' Coreopsis

The recent introduction **'Mercury Rising' PPAF**, from the BIG BANG™ Series of *Coreopsis*, sets a new standard and direction in breeding for hardy, large-flowered coreopsis in shades of maroon, red, pink and bi-tones. Its hybrid vigor makes it a fast-growing perennial, which, because it is sterile and sets no viable seed, flowers nonstop from early summer through autumn much like an annual, but with the added advantage of being hardy from Zones 5 to 9. Others in this series include 'Cosmic Evolution' with large, creamy white flowers suffused with magenta in cooler weather; 'Cosmic Eye' with petals of claret-red tipped in golden yellow; 'Full Moon' with enormous canary yellow flowers up to 2½ inches across; 'Galaxy', a semi- to fully double form of pure yellow; the fascinating and color-changing 'Redshift', whose flowers are butter yellow with a red eye in the heat of summer but take on more red coloration when temperatures drop; and 'Star Cluster' with creamy white petals stained purple at the base, the purple radiating through the petals in cooler weather.

'Pinwheel' Coreopsis

Unique in its flower form and also hardy to Zone 6 is *Coreopsis* 'Pinwheel', another recent introduction with distinctive fluted petals in the softest shade of buttery yellow, which are perfectly enhanced by its finely dissected blue-green foliage. Its heat and humidity tolerance and resistance to powdery mildew make it an excellent choice for the South, where others struggle.

■ **Improved cold hardiness** over previous selections that didn't live through the winter. Long season of bloom from early summer to frost. Flowers now come in a variety of colors, including yellows, red, pinks, and bicolors. **Good drainage is essential,** especially in winter. ■ **FULL SUN.** ■ **ZONES 5 TO 9,** depending on variety.

PURPLE CONEFLOWER

Plant This!

'Daydream' Coneflower

One of the most exciting developments in the world of coneflowers has been the introduction of varieties sporting flowers in beautiful shades of yellow. *Echinacea* **'Daydream'** is one of the most exceptional with large flowers on tall, sturdy stems perfect for cutting. The yellow coloration comes from a species called *Echinacea paradoxa*, which is a stunning plant in its own right.

The **purple coneflower**, *Echinacea purpurea*, is a plant that most gardeners, whether beginners or seasoned veterans, have a long and torrid affair with and rightly so. Its easy culture, tough disposition, and showy, long-lasting blooms have made it a garden favorite for generations. In the past decade, so many new varieties have been introduced to the market it is often difficult to know which ones to buy. New introductions expanded the color range from the standard pinkish purple into reds, oranges, yellows, and bicolors. New flower forms, including doubles and those with quilled or spooned petals, and an expanded range of plant sizes have helped reinvent this classic garden perennial.

'Pink Poodle' Coneflower

While not every gardener will fall in love with the more unusual forms such as **'Pink Poodle'**, their long-lasting flowers and full, ruffly blooms are an exciting addition to the garden. Because these "topknot" forms set very little seed, they flower for an extended period of time, sometimes blooming for more than two months in the summer border.

'Tomato Soup' Coneflower

One of the most surprising paths that many hybridizers have taken is in the search for a true red coneflower with deep, saturated color. 'Tomato Soup' comes as close as any, with flowers that open a rich, orangey red and slowly fade to a deep, reddish pink. This two-tone effect makes for a plant that positively glows in the garden.

An important cultural note: Because of their hybrid vigor and their ability to produce multiple flushes of blooms throughout the summer, even from a very young age, flowering stems of these new, vigorous hybrids should be removed from the plants at planting time and as soon as they reappear during their first growing season. This is a difficult task for many gardeners, but redirects the plant's energy back to its root system and helps to ensure that it will return again the following year and well into the future. Otherwise, new plants may, quite literally, flower themselves to death.

■ **Tough, durable, and very resilient** once established, coneflower is perfect for both beginning and experienced gardeners. Attractive to butterflies and beneficial pollinating insects. Coneflower makes an excellent, long-lasting cut flower. New hybrids come in a **vast array of colors.** ■ **FULL SUN.** ■ **ZONES 4 TO 9.**

SOLOMON'S SEAL

Plant This!

When it comes to **Solomon's seal** (*Polygonatum* species and cultivars), the market has been dominated by one plant for more than thirty years—*Polygonatum odoratum* 'Variegatum', the variegated Solomon's seal from Japan. This easy-to-grow and undemanding perennial remains popular for good reason. Its clean, green-and-white variegation lightens and brightens the shade garden, it's untouched by pests or disease, it looks good from emergence in spring until it goes dormant in autumn (and even has fall color!), and it makes a great cut stem for flower arranging. While it does spread by underground rhizomes, it is never invasive and is easy to dig and divide when necessary. A wide variety of exquisite species and select cultivars remain unexplored by most gardeners, but never fail to thrill those who discover them.

'Double Stuff' Solomon's Seal

A recent introduction to the market, **'Double Stuff'** is a vigorous selection with leaves whose white margins are double the width of the common variegated form, making it twice as bright and twice as showy as its common counterpart. A nearly identical selection, **'Double Wide'**, is also available, and the only real difference appears to be the source from which you buy them. Both are outstanding selections.

'Silver Lining' Solomon's Seal

A related species, *Polygonatum falcatum* differs from its more common counterpart in that it is of smaller stature all around—not as tall and with narrower leaves—but retains all of the grace and style of its larger-growing kin. A particularly attractive form most often sold as **'Silver Lining'** bears a broad, silvery stripe down the center of each leaf. The effect is refined and elegant, and is always good for a few "What's that?" remarks when gardening friends visit.

Once you have taken a few first steps with the Solomon's seal clan, it is almost inevitable that you will become a collector. Few plants are as easy or forgiving, with only the alpine species being troublesome outside of their preferred range, and even they are worth at least some effort. Other selections you might consider include *Polygonatum odoratum* **'Fireworks'**; *Polygonatum* x *hybridum* **'Grace Barker'**; *Polygonatum kingianum*, and the diminutive and charming *Polygonatum humile,* which no shade garden should be without.

■ Many Solomon's seals make fine **deciduous groundcovers,** spreading slowly to form large colonies over time. Mail-order nurseries carry a broad selection of the more unusual species and cultivars. Drought tolerant, but best in woodsy, moist soils. ■ **PART SUN TO SHADE.** ■ **ZONES 3 TO 8,** depending on species.

CHAPTER 3

Annuals

I f you ask gardeners how they feel about annuals, the responses are often equally divided between those who are all for planting annuals each season in the garden and those who feel it is either too much work, a waste of money, or both. I would argue that without annuals, gardeners are missing out on a tremendous group of plants whose often continuous color helps knit the garden together throughout the seasons, whether it's the pansies and violas of winter, the larkspur and breadseed poppies of spring, or the bright and colorful lantana mixed with various salvias, angelonia, and zinnias of summer and autumn.

When it comes to choosing annuals for the garden, the choice is often two-fold: one choice is whether or not to add something entirely new to the garden and give it a try, but more often, the choice is about new and improved varieties of old garden favorites that we've loved for years. Hybridizers are working nonstop to improve the color ranges, growth habits, pest and disease resistance, and much more of all of the most popular garden annuals. Throw in a few new and unusual species from around the world and the options can be mindboggling.

How, then, to decide which annuals are going to be the best for your garden? Which are going to provide the most flowers and the brightest color for the season ahead? Which will attract butterflies and other beneficial insects to the garden? What should you plant if you want plenty of blooms to cut and enjoy indoors on summer's hottest days? In the following pages, you'll find recommendations for the best of the best when it comes to annuals—the most desirable and improved forms of some classic garden plants that no garden should be without.

Plant This!

For the past decade, angelonia—*Angelonia* hybrids, also called summer snapdragon because the shape of its blooms bears some resemblance to the snapdragon flower—has been at the top of the popularity list for sun-loving annuals. Rightly so. Its durability and easy care make it the perfect choice for gardeners of every experience level. This entry is not so much about finding a replacement to plant *instead* of angelonia as it is to point gardeners in the right direction when choosing which of the many varieties of angelonia to add to their gardens or containers. Keep in mind that with new varieties entering the supply chain every season, older varieties may disappear as newer ones take their place.

Angelface® Blue Angelonia

My series of choice when it comes to angelonia is the **Angelface®** Series, part of the Proven Winners® family of plants. In addition to the original cobalt blue flowers of **Angelface® Blue**, the series has now been expanded to include **Angelface® Dark Violet, Angelface® White, Angelface® Dresden Blue, Angelface® Pink, Angelface® Wedgwood Blue**, and others. Angelonia love the heat and grow most vigorously, producing the most flowers when temperatures begin to soar. They thrive in the summer heat and humidity of the Southeast and Midwest, but perform equally well in milder climates. Angelonia's only real requirements are full sun, rich soil, and a little extra feeding from time to time to keep them flowering profusely throughout the summer.

Serena™ Angelonia

Slightly taller than their Angelface® counterparts, the **Serena™** Series is well suited to mixed plantings in beds and borders, as well as large containers. Long spires of colorful blooms appear throughout the summer on plants that are nearly 1½-foot tall. Looser and a little more wildflowery in its appearance, it makes a great addition to informal plantings where its habit allows it to mix and mingle in graceful beauty with neighboring plants. Colors in the series include **Serena™ Purple**, **Serena™ Lavender**, **Serena™ Lavender Pink**, **Serena™ White**, and at least two mixes.

New series appear on the market almost every year, making improvements on plant habit, bloom size, and range of color. Recent introductions include spreading varieties for low-growing, ever-blooming mats of color for planters, hanging baskets, or the front of the flowerbed.

■ Angelonia is an **easy, carefree, and free-flowering annual** that blooms from spring to frost. Regular watering and feeding throughout summer will keep angelonia blooming profusely. **No deadheading required** except to tidy up the plants. Size is 10 to 20 inches by 10 to 20 inches, depending on variety. ■ **FULL SUN.**

Plant This!

There is good news out there for gardeners! Today's garden centers carry an ever-expanding array of beautiful **begonias**, *Begonia semperflorens-cultorum*, that make perfect substitutes for the ubiquitous wax begonia that has spent the past forty years welcoming people to every shopping center, apartment complex, and industrial park across the nation. So you say you love begonias? Plant them! This is not to discourage the planting of begonias, but instead to encourage the planting of the very best begonias you can find. Modern breeding has transformed the begonia from a dumpy mound of half-burned leaves with colorful, but small blooms into the new grand dame of the garden with graceful growth habits, handsome foliage, and spectacular clusters of blooms.

BabyWing™ Begonia

If your preference runs to something a little more compact, but just as elegant and floriferous in the garden, the **BabyWing™** Series of begonias may be your new go-to annual. In those difficult transitional zones between sun and shade where it is too shady for sun-loving plants, but too sunny for the shade lovers, **BabyWing™** will fit right in! **BabyWing™ White Bronze Leaf** is particularly beautiful, with dark, bronzy green leaves that form a dramatic backdrop to show off the pure white blooms. Growing only 12 to 15 inches tall and wide, it is compact enough to use directly in place of the old-fashioned wax begonia, but graceful enough to lend itself as a focal point to pots and other containers. **BabyWing™ Pink** and **BabyWing™ White**, both with green leaves, round out the series.

■ **Very low maintenance,** no deadheading required. Drought tolerant and forgiving once established, but **prefer rich, well-drained soil and regular watering.** Mature size can vary greatly, 10 inches to 3 feet with a similar spread, depending on the variety you choose. ■ **FULL SUN TO SHADE,** depending on variety.

Bonfire® Begonia

Popular for hanging baskets and mixed pots because of its pendulous habit and nodding flowers in a luminescent shade of orange, the **Bonfire®** begonia (*Begonia boliviensis*) has also helped boost the popularity of begonias once again. Compact plants bear hundreds of brilliantly colored blooms throughout the summer. Newer colors include **Bonfire® Scarlet** and **Bonfire® Choc Red**.

Dragon Wing® Begonia

The transformation of the begonia began on a large scale with the introduction of the **Dragon Wing®** Series in the early 2000s. Originally only available in red, it now also comes in a very pleasing shade of pink, the glossy green wing-shaped leaves setting off both colors perfectly. Larger growing than many begonias, reaching 2 feet tall by 2 feet wide in warmer clients and slightly less where it's cooler, it quickly fills in open spaces in the shady garden or becomes the dramatic focal point of a container. Its arching, graceful stems bear large clusters of showy blooms that dangle from the plant like colorful earrings.

Plant This!

Beginning in the 1990s, a new plant that resembled a miniature petunia took the gardening world by storm. **Calibrachoa** (*Calibrachoa* hybrids) quickly became known by one of its trademark names, **Million Bells®**, loved for its profusion of tiny petunia-like blooms that completely covered the plants from spring through fall. It was soon discovered, however, that homeowners had a difficult time growing the plant and keeping it healthy due to its very specific pH requirements. Even the professionals struggled to grow it well. Specific nutritional needs were difficult to meet, special fertilizers were required, and growing the plants well was more trouble than most homeowners were willing to go to. Many were not successful, even if they gave it a valiant effort. A new hybrid solves this dilemma.

Supercal® Hybrid

The most recent breakthroughs in breeding with *Calibrachoa* involve crossing the very best of the hybrid petunias, which are vigorous and undemanding, with the very best of the calibrachoas, creating a super hybrid—x *Calitunia*—that combines the easy-to-grow nature and nonstop flowering of the former with the petite blooms and nearly limitless color range of the latter. Calibrachoa's fussy demands of perfect pH and constant feeding to keep them healthy and flowering have been nearly eliminated, while the strong roots of their petunia parents improve the new hybrids' resistance to root rot disease, which had plagued calibrachoas since their introduction a decade ago.

Several companies are busy breeding new forms with some of the best hybrids now being marketed and sold to gardeners as the **Supercal®** and **Calitunia®** Series, with many more on their way. Perfect for hanging baskets and for spilling over the edges of window boxes and pots, these new varieties require no deadheading, less feeding, and very little maintenance to keep them blooming throughout the summer. Perhaps their finest attribute, however, is the wide range of clean, pure colors that calibrachoa has brought to the petunia. Ranging from bright fuchsia and purple to clear reds, warm terra cottas, and refreshing oranges and yellows that were more or less unknown in petunias and their relatives prior to a few years ago, the **Supercal®**, **Calitunia®**, and future series will continue to expand the rainbow of colors gardeners have to choose from.

■ **Disease resistance** and tolerance of a wide pH range makes them easy to grow. Regular watering and feeding will keep them in top shape. **No deadheading required!** Size is 6 to 10 inches tall by 12 to 24 inches wide, depending on variety. ■ **FULL TO PART SUN.**

Plant This!

Cleome—*Cleome hasslerana*, also called spider flower—has been a charming member of cottage gardens for over a century. Its tall spires of white, pink, or lavender flowers grace mid- and late summer gardens with open, airy blooms, inviting hummingbirds and an assortment of moths and butterflies to feast on its nectar. As gardens have become smaller, however, gardeners now prefer newer, more compact varieties over some old-fashioned favorites. Often, I eschew this trend toward compactness, longing for the graceful old forms of annuals and perennials that were once available, but when it comes to cleome, I've become rather smitten with many of the new varieties. By midsummer, when the old-fashioned form becomes tall and rangy, these new cultivars shine, not missing a beat.

Senorita Rosalita™ Cleome

The current summit of cleome breeding reached its peak with the introduction of the **Senorita** Series. Just tall enough to be graceful and airy, but shrubby in habit, **Senorita Rosalita™** reaches 36 inches tall and as wide, bearing so many rosy pink blooms from midsummer to fall that they nearly obscure the plant. Its clean, pest-free leaves remain dark green and clothe the plant nearly to the ground. Best of all, that skunky odor and the thorns of the old-fashioned cleome have been eliminated. **Senorita Blanca®** is the second plant in the series with silvery white blooms on the same size plant. These plants are also sterile, eliminating the problem of seedlings taking over the garden, which the old-fashioned types were known for.

The introduction of several yellow-flowering species of *Cleome* and its close relatives are sure to change this old-fashioned cottage garden favorite even more as hybridizers work endlessly toward new and improved forms and colors. Perhaps one day we will see the color range expanded to include soft, buttery yellows and luscious peach tones in addition to the traditional lavender, pink, and white. Anything is possible!

Sparkler Series Cleome

One of the first trends toward more compact forms of cleome came with the introduction of the **Sparkler Series**, which bears, in abundance, the large white or lavender-pink flowers of the old-fashioned varieties on compact, shrubby plants with handsome, deep green foliage. New colors have made this series even more popular, with a deep rose pink and a softer true pink (without the lavender undertones) rounding out the group. Plants are available in garden centers in early spring and are often sold "in the green," meaning without flowers. This is when they are at their most vigorous and will transplant easily, with little shock or delay in growth. Flowering will begin with a few days to a few weeks and will continue on through autumn. The **Sparkler Series** is still widely available and should not be overlooked by gardeners who love the traditional look of cleome, but could live without its bare legs, yellowing leaves, and abundant seeding about the garden.

■ Newer forms are **compact, shrublike in habit, and flower nearly nonstop** from summer to frost. Many are nearly or completely sterile, reducing or eliminating the problem of reseeding. Drought tolerant once established. Size is 24 to 36 inches by 24 to 36 inches, depending on variety. ■ **FULL SUN.**

Plant This!

Gardeners everywhere remember the **old-fashioned coleus** (*Solenostemon* hybrids) grown by our mothers and grandmothers. Residents of the shade garden, most were grown from seed in an assortment of bright and exotic color combinations that brightened the spaces between hostas and ferns or formed compact hedges of riotous color down the edge of a shady walk. Deadheading was a constant job to keep the plants from flowering and going to seed, signaling the end of their annual "life" and their untimely midsummer demise. For gardeners trying to grow their own plants from seed each year, damping off a fungal disease was a constant concern with seedlings collapsing almost overnight and ruining that year's colorful crop. Thankfully, two decades worth of selection and breeding have changed the coleus forever.

'Gold Lace' Coleus

Coleus are still highly desirable for brightening up the shady corners of the garden too. Most garden centers today will specify which varieties thrive in sun and which prefer a shadier corner. If it's a bright splash of color you need to fill those empty places between the green of summer's hostas, ferns, and hellebores, coleus still do the trick and in a much improved manner over grandma's old-fashioned varieties.

■ New varieties have thicker leaves for **pest resistance and bright, nonfading colors.** Regular watering and feeding is required to keep them looking good. Size is 10 to 36 inches tall by 18 to 36 inches wide, depending on variety. ■ **FULL SUN TO PART SHADE.**

'Sedona' Coleus

In the early 1990s, two words—**sun coleus**—would free coleus from the garden's shady nooks and make it the focal point of beds and borders everywhere. Much of the breeding work that led to these new coleus and eventually to the selection and introduction of individual cultivars was done in Florida, where hot, humid summers and sunshine prevailed and the need for coleus that would withstand summer's onslaught was paramount. Plants were evaluated for color that would endure the hot summer sun without fading, for leaves that were thick and leathery that would not burn and scorch, and for plants that would thrive in heat and humidity. Cultivars such as **'Sedona'**, **'Alabama Sunset'**, **'Big Blonde'**, **'Redhead'**, **'Fishnet Stockings'**, **'Pineapple'**, and many more soon became regular residents of sunny beds and borders.

'Trailing Rose' Coleus

Soon after the debut of the sun coleus, work began on a group of coleus that would become known as trailing coleus. With a relaxed, sprawling habit, these plants remain low to the ground or trail gracefully over the side of a container, raised bed, or wall. Most will grow either in sun or shade, their color varying somewhat depending on their exposure. Favorite varieties include **'Trailing Plum'**, **'Trailing Rose'**, **'Chocolate Drop'**, and others.

Plant This!

There has been much talk over the past few years of **impatiens** (*Impatiens walleriana*) and the impatiens downy mildew disease that is plaguing plants across the country. This disease has nearly eliminated impatiens from many landscapes and sent professional growers, garden designers, and homeowners into a tailspin looking for alternatives to the bright and colorful blooms that impatiens once offered. But what is impatiens downy mildew and why is it such a problem? Impatiens downy mildew is a soil-borne disease that attacks the leaves of impatiens, causing them to yellow, curl, and eventually fall off, leaving nothing but bare stems and, eventually, dead plants. Unfortunately, the disease has infected many large growing operations that deliver plants across the country and this has only hastened the spread of the disease.

SunPatiens®

Fortunately, the common impatiens' close relatives—the **New Guinea impatiens** (*Impatiens hawkeri* hybrids) and the even newer **SunPatiens®**—are resistant to impatiens downy mildew. Though they require more sun than the common impatiens, both are excellent alternatives for areas that receive at least a half day of sun. **SunPatiens®** have been tested in climates as hot as Dallas, Texas, and have thrived—even in full sun—despite the heat and humidity. Flowers are larger than the common impatiens on both the **New Guinea impatiens** and **SunPatiens®**, and many varieties have uniquely colored or variegated leaves, creating striking color complements and contrasts between flowers and foliage.

■ New Guinea impatiens and SunPatiens® make excellent substitutes for common impatiens in shade gardens, beds, and borders. Both are unaffected by downy mildew, which is affecting common impatiens across the country. ■ Both New Guinea impatiens and SunPatiens® require some sun in order to thrive and bloom.

Wishbone Flower

Another old-fashioned garden plant that has seen a recent resurgence is **Torenia**, *Torenia* hybrids, the **wishbone flower**. A cottage garden favorite for many years, the plant fell out of favor amongst gardeners in many climates because it was often a weak grower and its small, blue-purple flowers, while beautiful, were best viewed up close and offered little impact at any distance. With new varieties being introduced each spring, the **Moon™ Series** is always a favorite. A unique breakthrough in breeding, this series offers colors never-before-seen in *Torenia*, including white, golden yellow, butter yellow, and a wide range of purples and blues in various shades and patterns. Plants are compact and flower profusely from spring through fall. Because they are sterile, no deadheading is required to keep them looking their best throughout the season.

■ Torenia, wishbone flower, is a **perfect substitute** for common impatiens in pots, planters, and other containers, or where low-growing plants are needed. The color range of wishbone flower has been expanded to pastel yellow, bright gold, and grape purple. Wishbone flower is not affected by downy mildew. ■ **PART SUN TO PART SHADE.**

INSTEAD OF
OLD-FASHIONED LANTANA

Plant This!

'Carlos' Lantana

Outside of the many new series that have and continue to be introduced, some very desirable individual selections are available to gardeners too. A longtime favorite is the variety **'Carlos'**, whose flower color and intensity can only be measured in megawatts when its new flowers, which open brightest golden orange, begin changing through shades of pink and fuchsia to deepest purple. **'Star Landing'**, with flowers in a bicolor combination of screaming golden orange and deep orange-red, make it a standout in the garden and **'Chapel Hill Yellow'** blooms in a not-too-harsh shade of bright yellow from early summer until frost. 'Star Landing' and 'Chapel Hill Yellow' are both hardy to Zone 7b and may be perennial in the South.

For gardeners everywhere, but especially in the South, **lantana** (*Lantana* species and hybrids) has long been one of the most popular annuals for locations where heat, humidity, and full sun are the order of the day. Old cultivars grew almost like groundcovers or, in the case of more upright varieties, shrubs, especially in hot climates. A single plant may have spread 5 feet or more by season's end or grown into a 3-foot by 3-foot bush (sometimes more) by the time frost finally arrived. This made lantana difficult to accommodate in smaller gardens or in areas where its habit of shouldering its way past neighboring plants was undesirable. And because its stems were often long and lanky, the floral display was sometimes sparse, bearing little impact in the landscape.

Landmark Series Lantana

Plant breeding is big business and nearly every major plant breeding company in the world has jumped into the lantana market with new series, new colors, and new forms being introduced at breakneck pace. Each spring it seems there are at least a dozen new varieties or series to choose from. It would be futile to try to cover them all here, so let's focus on a few of the best. For versatility and uniformity across the board, the **Landmark Series** has proven to be one of the finest. Starting with **'Landmark Yellow'** (shown), a compact and uniform variety that flowers nonstop from spring through frost, the series quickly expanded to include **'Landmark Citrus'**, which has won rave reviews from both professional and home gardeners, as well as **'Landmark Sunrise Rose'**, **'Landmark Peach Sunrise'**, **'Landmark White'**, and more. These plants set little seed, meaning little or no deadheading is required and their flowers sit atop the foliage for outstanding visual impact.

■ **Excellent for attracting butterflies, hummingbirds, and pollinators** to the garden. Some varieties may be perennial in the South, hardy to Zone 7. **Extremely drought tolerant** and will flower even under adverse conditions. Size is 1 to 3 feet tall by 2 to 6 feet wide, depending on climate and variety. ■ **FULL SUN.**

Plant This!

Gardeners up north have long used the bright, almost cobalt blue blooms of **lobelia**, *Lobelia erinus*, as vivid accents along garden paths, bed edges, and cascading out of pots and window boxes. Dainty, red-tinged foliage plays in perfect harmony with the glowing blue blossoms to dramatic and stunning effect. The problem? Lobelia is a mild-climate plant, thriving where summers are short and cool and where nighttime temperatures drop reliably to give the plants a break from daytime heat. In the South, lobelia was little more than a fleeting dream to be enjoyed for a few weeks in spring before succumbing to the oppressive heat and humidity of summer. In shaded containers, perhaps it would remain until midsummer, though rarely looking its best.

Laguna™ Sky Blue Lobelia

Heat tolerance has been the greatest "invention" when it comes to the new lobelia hybrids that grace our gardens today. Where the old-fashioned lobelia simply curled up and died when summer got too hot, hybrids such as the **Laguna™ Series** have finally beaten the heat and will continue flowering everywhere throughout the hot summer months and well into autumn. Not only are they heat tolerant, but they require no deadheading and they come in several shades of the ever-elusive blue that gardeners everywhere are so keen on. **Laguna™ Sky Blue** is just what the name says—the most sumptuous shade of sky blue. **Laguna™ Heavenly Lilac** and **Laguna™ White** are the softer colors in the series, while **Laguna™ Compact Blue With Eye** is a bi-colored form with bright blue flowers highlighted by a white central eye.

Lucia® Lavender Blush Lobelia

If dramatic waterfalls of blue flowers are what you're after, consider the **Lucia® Series** of lobelia. Grown for its trailing habit up to 24 inches long, it will tumble out of pots, planters, and window boxes to create cascades of luscious deep blue or lavender blue blooms. The two varieties in the series so far are **Lucia® Dark Blue** and **Lucia® Lavender Blush** with other colors sure to come in the future. As with the **Laguna™** Series, **Lucia®** was bred for heat tolerance and vigor, making it easy for the home gardener no matter what climate they may garden in, and because it's sterile, no deadheading is required to keep it blooming and looking its best throughout the summer.

■ New hybrids are **heat and humidity tolerant,** no deadheading required. Compact forms are good for edging beds and borders. Trailing forms tumble over the edges of pots, planters, and window boxes. Size is 6 to 10 inches tall by 12 to 24 inches wide. ■ **FULL SUN TO PART SHADE.**

Plant This!

Depending on where you live and garden, **pansies** (*Viola* x *wittrockiana*) can either be winter-blooming annuals that are planted in the fall or spring and early summer-blooming annuals that are planted in early spring. From Zone 6 southward into the warmer zones, pansies are commonly planted in autumn to grow and produce colorful blooms through most or all of the often-dreary months of winter. They will continue to flower throughout the following spring until hot summer weather arrives, when they are replaced with heat-loving annuals. North of Zone 6, pansies are enjoyed in spring and early summer. The problem with pansies is that they are often finicky and high maintenance, requiring regular watering, feeding, and deadheading—even in winter—in order to look their best.

■ Perfect for adding **touches of winter color** to the garden in warmer zones. Violas have smaller flowers than pansies, but produce up to ten times as many blooms. Where they are used for winter planting, watering is important on warm, dry days. Size is 6 inches tall by 12 inches wide. ■ **FULL SUN.**

Sorbet™ Series Viola

Violas, on the other hand, are as easy and low maintenance as almost any plant can be. Planting times coincide with their close cousins, the pansies—autumn in the South for winter and early spring blooms and spring in the North for spring and early summer blooms. Some gardeners worry that because the flowers on violas are so much smaller than pansies, they will be less showy in the garden. Nothing could be further from the truth. The **Sorbet™ Series** is particularly hardy and the plants cover themselves with blooms from the time they're planted until hot weather finally gets the best of them. Violas truly offer a rainbow of colors from some of the purest blues to deep, golden yellows, reds, oranges, and an array of hues in between, with faces or without.

'Ultima Morpho' Viola

Plant breeders working with both pansies and violas have created a new class of flowers sometimes referred to as "panolas." Whether you think of them as small-flowered pansies or large-flowered violas is up to you, but what you'll find for sure is that they combine the best attributes of both parents, with the hardiness of the violas and the larger blooms of the pansies. **'Ultima Morpho'** is a particular favorite in this category, bearing large (for a viola) flowers in a luminous shade of light blue, broadly marked with a clear yellow face and tiny black whiskers. Often, shades of bronze will also appear in the flowers, providing a stunning accent color.

This is only the tip of the iceberg when it comes to the many varieties of violas available on the market today. We've come a long way from the "Johnny jump-ups" of yesteryear, and there are very few that aren't colorful and welcome additions to the garden.

Plant This!

Pentas—sometimes called Egyptian starflower (*Pentas lanceolata*)—are another of those old-fashioned flowers that fell by the wayside for a number of years until new and improved hybrids revived their popularity over the past decade or two. Old cultivars had leggy growth habits that made blooms appear sparse and unimpressive, and they required near-constant deadheading to keep them flowering. Their color range was limited to shades of pink, most of which were muddy and unattractive, and occasionally white or red, which weren't much better. While they were still attractive to butterflies and hummingbirds, they weren't as attractive to gardeners who left them to live out their days in exile in the wilder parts of the garden.

'Butterfly Lavender' Pentas

One of the first series that helped revive the popularity of pentas as garden plants was the **Butterfly Series**. These were a breakthrough in pentas because they were grown from seed, yet still produced very uniform plants with clean, clear colors that delighted gardeners and butterflies alike. Flowers formed at the tops of the stems instead of between the leaves, making them showier in the garden, and the broad range of colors that were developed, including deep pink, white, red, blush pink, deep rose, and lavender, were better than any that had been offered up to that point and still rank near the top today. In warm climates, plants may reach 24 to 30 inches tall with stems long enough for cutting, but they are sturdy enough to hold the flowers firmly upright.

'Graffiti' Pentas

If an even more compact plant is what you're looking for, the **Graffiti Series** of pentas may be just what you seek. Perfect for bed edges and the front of the border plantings, it still bears the same gorgeous flowers in clusters 3 to 4 inches across, but on stocky, sturdy plants that remain between 12 and 18 inches tall. The flowers are borne in great abundance across the top of the plants, making them full of color throughout the summer. The **Graffiti Series** is available in few colors—red, violet, white, and pink—but the colors are clean and vibrant with no hint of the muddiness that plagued the old-fashioned varieties.

If you are a butterfly gardener or wish to attract beneficial pollinators to your garden, pentas ranks in the top five plants to do just that. On a warm summer day, few other plants in the garden will be as covered with butterflies and other beneficial insects as pentas.

■ **One of the top five** plants for **attracting butterflies and beneficial insects** to the garden. Thrives in heat and humidity. Needs regular watering, fertilizing, and deadheading for profuse flowering. Size is 1 to 3 feet tall by 1 to 3 feet wide, depending on variety. ■ **FULL SUN.**

OLD-FASHIONED PETUNIA

Plant This!

If you consider it, petunias (*Petunia* hybrids) really are where the annual revolution began. The introduction of the **Wave™ Series** was groundbreaking, and the hybridizing that has followed has changed the plant and the way we grow it forever. For the first time, petunias thrived in the heat and humidity without stretching and becoming weedy-looking, and their flowers maintained their color and size throughout the summer without fading or diminishing. Old-fashioned petunias, especially in hot summer climates, just couldn't keep up. No more constant deadheading and pinching to keep the plants producing more blooms. No more hoping for a short break in the weather that would revive the bedraggled plants lining the front walk in midsummer. No more half-dead hanging baskets by the front door. Hooray!

Supertunia® Vista Bubblegum

Following hot on the heels of the **Wave™** Series (see the next section) were a multitude of other series and novelty types that have only added to the petunia's continued popularity. The **Supertunia®** Series offers an enormous range of colors on nearly maintenance-free plants that require only regular watering and feeding to look their best. **Supertunia® Vista Bubblegum** is the best of the best, with shocking pink flowers that completely obscure the foliage from the time it's planted until the hardest frosts knock them back in late autumn. For novelty types, **Supertunia® Pretty Much Picasso** and **Supertunia® Picasso in Pink** are unique in that they have green edges to their purple or pink flowers, giving them quite the artistic flair.

Tidal Wave™ Petunia

If there were, indeed, a petunia revolution, we owe nearly all of it to one plant, the petunia now called **Wave™ Purple Classic**. It all began when that single plant took the gardening world by storm when it was introduced. Its low, groundcovering habit was new and revolutionary in the world of annuals, and when combined with the fact that it thrived in summer's heat and humidity without missing a beat *and* required no deadheading, it was destined for overnight success. Its only problem, if it had one, was that perhaps it was *too* vigorous. Today,

the groundhugging waves are joined by several others in the series, including **Shock Wave™** and **Easy Wave™**. Both have a more mounding habit and slightly less spread than the original **Wave™** selections, while **Tidal Wave™** delivers huge quantities of bloom on plants that roll across the garden at 24 inches tall with a 36-inch or greater spread. The most recent introduction to the family is **Double Wave™**, producing fully double, camellia or roselike blossoms on low, spreading plants.

■ Most new hybrids are sterile, requiring **no deadheading**. Leggy plants can be cut back by half, fertilized, and watered regularly to promote new growth and blooms. Excellent as blooming groundcovers or as cascading accents in baskets or planters. Size is 8 to 18 inches tall by 24 to 48 inches wide. ■ **FULL SUN.**

RED SALVIA

Plant This!

'Mystic Spires' Salvia

Some of the greatest improvements in annual salvias have come in the form of more compact plants that are easier to accommodate in today's smaller gardens and in varieties that flower nonstop throughout the summer months instead of cycling through periods of tremendous bloom followed by periods of tremendous boredom. **'Mystic Spires'** is the perfect example of a salvia whose compact, but still graceful form and continual flowering make it indispensible in perennial borders where its foot-long spires of indigo blue blooms fit right in and carry on long after many perennials have finished.

Fire engine red spikes of tubular blooms against dark green, pleated leaves bring back many memories of grandma's garden, where butterflies and hummingbirds fluttered around the **red salvia** (*Salvia splendens*) on summer afternoons. For many years, it was the only salvia available at garden centers, and when you asked for salvia, red salvia is what you were sold. That began to change with the introduction of the mealycup sage—*Salvia farinacea,* called 'Victoria Blue,' about thirty years ago—and slowly but surely, salvias have been on an upward trend ever since. The *Salvia* genus is a fairly large group of plants that range from the tropics to the cold northern plains; there are varieties suited to nearly every garden, some hardy perennials and some tender annuals. It is those annual types this section covers.

'Wendy's Wish' Salvia

For gardeners in the South, many of the old-fashioned salvias simply wouldn't hold up. Newer hybrids such as **'Wendy's Wish'** have been selected not only for their ability to flower from spring until frost, but also to withstand the brutal heat and humidity of summers in the South and along the East Coast. **'Wendy's Wish'** bears long spires of tubular flowers in a shocking shade of raspberry pink, attracting hummingbirds from every corner of the garden. Like 'Mystic Spires', its growth and bloom habit lends itself perfectly to inclusion in perennial beds, where no one will know that it's an annual unless you tell them. There, it will weave its way politely in and around its neighbors, creating stunning color and textural combinations with other plants and flowers.

If salvias simply aren't to your liking, consider planting **angelonia**, covered earlier in this chapter (see page 82). Its upright spires of blooms give a similar effect in the garden and its low-maintenance nature, long season of bloom, and lavender to deep blue color make it a perfect substitute.

■ One of the best plants for **attracting hummingbirds.** New hybrids are low maintenance, but **should be deadheaded for best flowering.** Annual salvias respond well to regular watering and fertilizing. Available in a variety of sizes, from small to large. ■ **FULL SUN TO PART SUN.**

Plant This!

Rows of **zinnias** (*Zinnia elegans*), often planted in the vegetable garden, take many of us back to our childhood days and memories of parents' or grandparents' gardens, vases full of brightly colored blooms on a kitchen windowsill or bathroom sink. Those same images might also bring back memories of plants turning white with powdery mildew by summer's end or leaves and petals chewed by a variety of pests. Nonetheless, the zinnia has survived, even in its old form. The new hybrids, though, are what have captured gardeners' attention of late and with good reason. The tall, lanky, and mildew-covered plants of old are no more, and while there is good argument to still grow a few for cutting, perhaps they are best left in an out-of-the-way corner.

Zahara™ Fire Zinnia

When it comes to modern hybrid zinnias, few can outperform the **Zahara™ Series**. Combining the very best attributes of the old-fashioned types with more disease- and pest-resistant species such as *Zinnia linearis*, the **Zahara™** clan bears large (for the type) blooms up to 2 inches in diameter and in such profusion that they almost hide the foliage. **Zahara™ Fire**, with its scarlet flowers suffused with gold and orange, is a high-impact plant no matter where it's planted, while **Zahara™ Yellow** is a pleasing shade of pure yellow that will fit into any color scheme. Other colors include red, cherry, white, coral, and the stunning **Zahara™ Starlight Rose**, each white bloom marked with a perfect cherry pink starburst at its center.

The **Profusion Series** is similar, with even narrower leaves, exceptional disease resistance, and small, starlike flowers in yellow, orange, gold, and white.

■ **Avoid overhead watering,** especially at night, to control fungal diseases. **Extremely drought tolerant once established** and good for areas that experience summer water restrictions. Regular deadheading and feeding will keep plants lush and flowering profusely. Size varies depending on the variety. ■ **FULL SUN.**

'Zowie' Zinnia

If you still love to grow your zinnias from seed, watching the tiny first leaves push through the soil and develop into healthy, vigorous plants full of brightly colored blooms, **'Zowie' zinna** fits the bill. With a seed strain that is also an All-America Selections winner, these zinnias have the brightly colored flowers with deep rose in the center blending into brilliant red, tipped with golden yellow. Extremely disease resistant and growing 2 to 3 feet tall, these make a perfect addition to beds and borders, and the long stems make 'Zowie' zinnias outstanding for cutting.

CHAPTER 4

Trees

When selecting trees for your landscape, you will make some very important choices in regards to your outdoor environment and the exterior of your home. Whether you're starting from scratch with a blank canvas to create the garden of your dreams or making changes to an already existing space, the trees you choose and how they grow will affect all other gardening you intend to do. The same choices will influence how efficiently your home is heated and cooled based on where the trees cast shade or allow the sun to shine through. Tree choice and location will also help determine where permanent features of the landscape, such as driveways, parking areas, patios, decks, and swimming pools, might be located in relation to how the shade of a tree's canopy or the encroachment of its roots might have certain advantages or consequences.

Unfortunately, tree selection is often based solely on how a tree looks—its ornamental value. This is how, in the 1980s, we ended up with subdivisions full of Bradford pears, based on looks alone. Thirty years later, these trees have reached the end of their useful lives and are found splitting in half, landing on cars and houses with little or no warning, and homeowners are literally paying the price.

Trees, for the most part, are as permanent as any building or structure on your property and should be chosen with that in mind. In addition to their practical applications and the beauty they provide, trees, as they grow and mature, add to the monetary value of your property. In the following pages, you'll find recommendations for the replacement of problem trees, as well as new and unusual forms of some of the most desirable ornamental and shade trees.

INSTEAD OF
CALLERY PEAR

Plant This!

Familiar to most gardeners by the name Bradford pear, Bradford is actually one specific variety in a group of plants that are either selections or hybrids of **callery pear**, *Pyrus calleryana*. Popular because of their fast rate of growth, spring flowers, and red fall color, they are now known for being weak-wooded with a propensity to split. In recent years, trees that were once thought to be sterile have begun setting copious quantities of seed and have been placed on the invasive exotic species rosters in many states. In some regions, the fast-growing, thorny, and undesirable "wild" form of the tree, most obvious when the trees bloom in spring, are overtaking entire forests.

'Autumn Blaze' Red Maple

For fast growth, durability, and spectacular fall color, few trees can rival the newer selections of red maple like **'Autumn Blaze'**. A hybrid between two native species, it combines the beauty and durability of the red maple with the fast growth rate of the silver maple, making for a marriage made in horticultural heaven. Because of its native parentage, there is little cause for concern about the tree seeding into the natural environment, should the occasional seedling appear. Other varieties of red maple that are worthy of consideration include 'Armstrong', 'Autumn Flame', 'October Glory', and 'Red Sunset'. All were selected for their outstanding and long-lasting displays of red fall color.

■ 'Autumn Blaze' maple can be used in the same way as callery pear in the landscape, as specimen trees, property boundaries, and as an **attractive tree for lining a drive.** ■ FULL SUN. ■ ZONES 3 TO 9.

'Autumn Brilliance' Serviceberry

If it's the white flowers of the callery pear's spring show you love, why not plant native serviceberry or one of its hybrid offspring? **'Autumn Brilliance'** (*Amelanchier* x *grandiflora*) provides white spring blooms followed by red berries beloved by wildlife and the same deep, ruby red color in late autumn that so many associate with the flowering pears that now dominate our gardens. Growing the trees in the open landscape rather than as understory trees allows them to fully develop and reach their greatest potential. When grown in the shade of taller trees, they always seem a little weak and bent, but when they are planted in the sun and free to grow unencumbered by surrounding trees, they can be beautiful!

■ Serviceberry is a smaller growing tree, but **highly ornamental** and useful as a smaller focal point or understory planting. **Berries are beloved by wildlife** and attract a tremendous range of birds to the garden as they ripen. ■ **FULL SUN TO PART SUN.** ■ **ZONES 4 TO 8.**

COLORADO BLUE SPRUCE

Plant This!

The dramatic, silvery blue color of the best forms of *Picea pungens*, the **Colorado spruce** (also called blue spruce or Colorado spruce), have made it a popular choice with homeowners for many decades. Mature specimens clothed in the bluest of blue needles are most impressive and some might even say revered in landscapes across the northern tier of states and the mountains of the West. Like many mountain-dwelling species, though, they are not always well suited to every climate. This is particularly true of the hot and humid South and along the eastern seaboard where spider mites are especially problematic during the summer months and heavy clay soils that remain wet for long periods of time cause a variety of root problems.

Blue Atlas Cedar

In warmer climates, where Colorado blue spruce suffers from heat, humidity, and a variety of other problems, **blue atlas cedar** (*Cedrus atlantica* 'Glauca') is just what the doctor ordered for adding that silvery blue color to the landscape. With evergreen needles similar in size, shape, and color to the best blue forms of the Colorado spruce, it is the answer to gardeners' prayers in Zone 7 and warmer, where the spruces suffer. Young plants may be open and rangy in appearance when first planted, but once established will quickly fill in to form upright, pyramidal specimens that with time will become some of the most magnificent trees in the landscape.

Golden Deodar Cedar

Similar in overall appearance to the blue atlas cedar, but with a fuller habit and golden yellow new growth in spring and early summer, is the **golden deodar cedar** (*Cedrus deodara* 'Aurea'). Faster growing than one might expect in its youth, it quickly forms an impressive specimen that only becomes more imposing and remarkable with age.

While it doesn't offer the year-round blue color of the others, its deep green needles tipped in golden yellow lend a soft glow to the landscape throughout the year. Silvery green forms do exist, **'Kashmir'** and **'Shalimar'** being two of the best, but neither matches the blue coloration of the best spruces.

■ In warm climates, atlas or deodar cedar are two of the **best alternatives to Colorado blue spruce.** Young trees may grow 2 to 3 feet per year, forming impressive specimens in under ten years. ■ **FULL SUN.** ■ Atlas cedar is the hardier of the two, to **ZONE 6.** Deodar cedar is hardy to **ZONE 7.**

Plant This!

Introduced into cultivation in 1750, the **eastern cottonwood** (*Populus deltoides*) has been a popular landscape tree ever since. In pioneer days, its tall, straight trunks stood as beacons on the prairie, signaling to travelers that water was nearby since it often grew in river bottoms, along stream banks, and at the edges of ponds and lakes. Being easy to transplant and grow made it popular then and is one of the reasons for its continued popularity today. When you get down to the heart of the matter, though, the eastern cottonwood, as stately and majestic as it may appear, is really a troubled tree. It is weak wooded, often breaking up in storms, and its messy habit of dropping twigs, branches, flowers, and fruit makes it undesirable for modern landscapes.

Dawn Redwood

Another fast-growing, but sturdy and long-lived tree, the **dawn redwood**, *Metasequoia glyptostroboides*, is one of the finest choices for today's landscapes. In warmer climates with longer growing seasons, it may grow as much as 5 to 6 feet per year in its youth, slowing down and becoming more structural and stately as it ages. Its soft, feathery leaves remind one of a hemlock or other evergreen, but in late fall those leaves turn a spectacular shade of russet-orange, persist for several days, and then fall to the ground. Again, a larger tree is probably not suited for the smallest subdivision lots, but where you have the space to grow a true specimen tree, few are more beautiful.

■ A fast-growing and sturdy tree, also growing quite large with age. It is best suited to larger yards and landscapes. Fall color can be spectacular, in an unusual shade of russet orange. Once thought to be extinct, it was rediscovered in China in 1944. ■ **FULL SUN. ■ ZONES 4 TO 8.**

Tulip Poplar

Some may argue that **tulip poplar,** *Liriodendron tulipifera*, is simply an even trade with the eastern cottonwood—that perhaps it doesn't have any more redeeming qualities about it than the tree it's intended to replace. I disagree. For a fast-growing tree, the tulip poplar is actually quite durable, and where you need a good tree, fast, tulip poplar fills the bill. Growing 3 feet or more a year, a 10-year-old specimen can easily reach 30 to 35 feet with a 20- to 25-foot spread. That's a good bit of shade in a pretty short amount of time, all things considered. Its growth rate coupled with its very attractive habit, its uniquely shaped leaves, and, when it's old enough, its green and pale orange tulip-shaped flowers (hence, the name) makes a more than satisfying landscape tree. It does grow large, so is probably not well suited to the smallest properties.

■ Fast-growing and becoming very large over time, tulip poplar is best suited to larger yards and landscapes. Around age ten it will begin producing its **beautiful goblet-shaped blooms** reminiscent of tulips. ■ Deep rooted and providing high, dappled shade, it allows other plants to grow easily underneath it. ■ **FULL SUN.** ■ **ZONES 4 TO 9.**

Eastern white pine (*Pinus strobus*) has long been the go-to plant for quick and easy evergreen screens and windbreaks from Zone 3 in the North to Zone 8 in the South. Its soft, feathery needles, fast rate of growth, and exceptional adaptability supported its popularity in the landscape for more than 100 years. Recently, though, white pine blister rust, which infects the bark and eventually kills the tree; white pine weevil, which kills the terminal shoots; and pine tip moth, which does the same, have all become serious problems for the white pine, causing it to die, sometimes *en masse*, throughout its range. Unfortunately, many species of pine are suffering from the same or similar pests and diseases and suitable alternatives are becoming harder to find.

Plant This!

Norway Spruce

It may seem unusual to recommend a spruce in place of a pine, but the **Norway spruce** (*Picea abies*) because of its deep green color, similar habit of growth, and adaptability from North to South makes it a more than acceptable substitute. As a young plant, it is relatively fast growing, upright, and pyramidal. With age, the base broadens out to impressive proportions. The weight of the limbs causes the tree to take on a graceful, semiweeping form that is stately and elegant in the landscape, giving a great sense of age and maturity. Hardy from Zones 2 to 7, it is as adaptable as nearly any other conifer, requiring only full sun and rich, *well-drained* soil—no spruce likes wet feet!

■ Norway spruce is hardy and adaptable to a wide range of conditions. Norway spruce is more **tolerant of cold winter winds** and a better choice for windbreaks or planting in open areas. It will become broad spreading at the base as it matures.
■ **FULL SUN.** ■ **ZONES 2 TO 7.**

'Yoshino' Japanese Cedar

Since pines are largely out of the question as replacements for other pines, we must turn to other types of evergreens for substitutes. **Japanese cedar** (*Cryptomeria japonica*) is one such plant. The cultivar **'Yoshino'** is a handsome form that is being made more widely available to homeowners by enterprising nursery owners and retail centers, which have seen the need for alternative forms of evergreens for the landscape. Its bright green needles turn an attractive shade of bronze in winter and its fast rate of growth makes it excellent for screening. It maintains its graceful, pyramidal shape for many years, much like the white pine does in its youth. One of the most adaptable conifers, it will grow from Zone 5 (as far north as Boston) well into the subtropical regions of Zone 9.

▨ Japanese cedar is hardy and **adaptable to a wide range of conditions.** It benefits from some moisture at its roots. It may need protection from harsh winter winds to avoid drying and wind burn. 'Yoshino' Japanese cedar remains upright as it ages. ▨ **FULL SUN TO PART SUN.** ▨ **ZONES 5 TO 9.**

INSTEAD OF
FLOWERING DOGWOOD

Plant This!

'Appalachian Spring' Flowering Dogwood

Disease-resistant selections of the native dogwood have been made in recent years with the cultivar **'Appalachian Spring'**, discovered in Catoctin Mountain Park, Maryland, and tested extensively for resistance to anthracnose at the University of Tennessee prior to its release in 1998, leading the way. It has also been used in several breeding programs to introduce disease resistance into native dogwood species in the hopes that future introductions will be resistant or possibly even immune to the anthracnose disease.

One of the most popular native ornamental trees, the **flowering dogwood** (*Cornus florida*) lights up the edges of forests and woodlands each spring with its white or occasionally pink blooms. In many locations, though, the dogwood has suffered tremendously from a serious disease called **dogwood anthracnose**. Once infected, trees will slowly succumb, and while the disease is not necessarily lethal, it can be disfiguring. In addition to anthracnose, powdery mildew is a common affliction on dogwoods, particularly in the hot and humid Southeast. Fortunately, a number of disease-resistant selections of native dogwood have been made in recent years, and ornamental species from other parts of the world are much less susceptible.

■ Rutgers University's hybrid dogwoods are **resistant to both anthracnose and powdery mildew**. Chinese or Kousa dogwood is also highly disease resistant. It requires full sun, even in the South, for peak growth and flowering. ■ *Cornus florida:* **FULL TO PART SUN. ZONES 5 TO 8.** ■ *Cornus kousa* and its hybrids: **FULL SUN. ZONES 4 TO 8.**

Chinese or Kousa Dogwood

Essentially immune to dogwood anthracnose, the **Chinese dogwood** (*Cornus kousa*) has been used extensively in the disease-resistant hybrids, but it is an excellent garden addition in its own right. Flowering about one month after native flowering dogwood, it extends the flowering season into mid- and late spring, bearing its creamy white blooms on the topside of branches that grow nearly parallel to the ground on mature specimens, creating a spectacular show. Large, fleshy, bright red fruits that resemble raspberries follow the flowers, extending the tree's show well into late summer and autumn.

Stellar Series® Dogwood

In the early 1990s the first cultivars in the **Stellar Series®** of dogwoods from the breeding program of Dr. Elwin Orton of Rutgers University were released to nursery trade and eventually made their way into nurseries and garden centers. This breakthrough in breeding involved creating hybrids between native **flowering dogwood** and the **Chinese** or **Kousa dogwood**, which is highly resistant to both anthracnose and powdery mildew. Selections such as **Stellar Pink®**, **Constellation®**, **Celestial®**, and **Ruth Ellen®** are now widely available and make hardy and disease-resistant additions to any landscape.

INSTEAD OF
GINKGO

Plant This!

Ginkgo (*Ginkgo biloba*) is a popular ornamental landscape tree and in many ways is a perfect choice for the modern landscape. Its relatively fast rate of growth, unique architectural form, and breathtaking fall color make it a top choice of landscape designers and homeowners alike. It has only one small problem. Female trees, if you're unlucky enough to have one, bear copious quantities of soft, sticky fruit in autumn—and they stink! No, really. They smell like bad cheese, and when there are enough of them, it can truly be stomach-turning. What to do then? Make sure, if you choose ginkgo as a landscape tree, that you purchase only male cultivars—there are plenty of them—that don't bear fruit.

'Autumn Gold' Ginkgo

There are a number of male ginkgos on the market today, all of which are fruitless, since only the female trees bear fruit. These are propagated by cuttings or grafts, so they are guaranteed to be true to type, whereas trees grown from seed cannot be determined to be male or female until they begin flowering or fruiting, and by then, it's too late. **'Autumn Gold'** is a fine male variety that is virtually pest free, tolerant of a wide range of soil types, and quite drought tolerant, once established. Its consistent and dramatic golden yellow fall color is one of its most desirable traits, lighting up the autumn landscape as it prepares to drop its leaves for winter.

■ Male selections do not bear fruit. **A wide variety of sizes and forms are available,** making the ginkgo suitable for nearly every landscape, large or small. Dwarf forms are outstanding garden accents and can be made into beautiful, bonsai-like specimens. ■ **FULL SUN.** ■ **ZONES 3 TO 8.**

Variegated Ginkgo

In addition to the standard ginkgo, whose uniquely shaped green leaves are interesting enough on their own, there are several varieties that have been selected for even more ornamental character, including dwarf forms that make beautiful accents for small gardens and variegated types whose leaves are striped in shades of cream and gold. **'Majestic Butterflies'** was selected for its highly variegated green-and-yellow-striped leaves. In autumn, the green sections of the leaves turn yellow, while the yellow stripes turn white, creating an even more dramatic effect when viewed up close. Dwarf forms, such as **'Gnome'** and **'Chase Manhattan'**, thrill collectors and add unique and unusual interest to even the smallest gardens or courtyards, while threadleaf or tube-leafed forms such as **'Tubiformis'** add exciting and highly unusual textural interest to the landscape.

LEYLAND CYPRESS

Plant This!

W here it's hardy, **Leyland cypress** (x *Cupressocyparis leylandii*) has become highly popular—to the point of being overused—for its tremendously fast rate of growth and its ability to provide evergreen screening between neighbors, to cover unsightly views, and to provide privacy or windbreaks in a very short period of time. Like many plants that are densely planted and highly overused, it has developed a number of fairly serious problems that make it less desirable for use in the landscape, not the least of which is its susceptibility to several canker and root rot diseases that can kill individual specimens or entire plantings seemingly overnight and with little that can be done about it by the time it's discovered.

'Emerald' Arborvitae

Many homeowners plant Leyland cypress not understanding their ultimate size, which is much larger than anyone might expect. Often, they are seen covering the front of a home, blocking a door or passageway, or completely engulfing an outbuilding because they were planted too close to an existing structure when they were small. **'Emerald' arborvitae** is a terrific choice where evergreen accents or screening are desired, but space is limited. Its narrow, conical form makes it great for tight spaces, and its ultimate size of just 15 feet high by 4 to 5 feet wide makes it a better fit for most landscapes.

While they are perhaps not suited to long hedges or windbreaks, there are some colorful golden or variegated forms of arborvitae that make outstanding focal points in the landscape, and new dwarf types, with a variety of foliage colors and forms, are wonderful accent plants for the garden.

'Green Giant' Arborvitae

'Green Giant' arborvitae is an exceptional alternative to the Leyland cypress, where evergreen screening and a fast rate of growth are desired. It is not uncommon to see 3 to 5 feet of growth per year from established plants, given full sun, well-prepared soil, and regular watering during the growing season. Rarely susceptible to the root rot diseases that plague Leyland cypress, it is a much more suitable choice for the landscape.

Unlike many arborvitae that are known for turning an undesirable bronzy brown during the winter months, **'Green Giant'** maintains its deep green foliage color throughout the year. It should be noted that like Leyland cypress, **'Green Giant'** does grow large, reaching 45 to 50 feet tall with a 20-foot spread at maturity. Place them wisely with that in mind.

Arborvitae comes in a **wide variety of habits and colors.** Larger-growing varieties resemble Leyland cypress. 'Green Giant' is the fastest growing and most similar in size to Leyland cypress. Arborvitae is **not susceptible to the root problems of Leyland cypress.** **FULL SUN.** **ZONES 3 TO 8,** depending on variety.

NORWAY MAPLE

Plant This!

In the North, Norway maple (*Acer platanoides*) was and still is to a certain degree, one of the most widely planted landscape trees around. This was due, in part, to its nearly indestructible nature and its ability to withstand extreme conditions, be they cold temperatures, sand or clay, acid or alkaline soil, or pollution. If its durability was one half of the equation, then the beauty of certain cultivars such as 'Crimson King', with its rich, maroon-colored leaves, certainly comprised the other half. Beauty and durability aside, the tree does have its problems. Shallow roots cover the soil surface, making it impossible to grow lawn or groundcover within their reach, and large anchor roots frequently buckle sidewalks, driveways, and even roads. It has also invaded native forests.

'October Glory' Red Maple

One of the finest alternatives to the Norway maple is the native **red maple** (*Acer rubrum*) or better yet, one of its outstanding cultivars such as **'October Glory'** or **'Red Sunset'**. Since both are selections of native species, reseeding into surrounding woodlands or wild areas is of little concern. **'Red Sunset'** is slightly better suited to gardens north of Zone 7, while **'October Glory'** will perform well into Zone 8, where it colors up reliably in the autumn even without the benefit of very cold temperatures. Both are relatively fast-growing, free from pests, and make durable and beautiful landscape trees.

A similar tree that is especially well suited to northern gardens is the **'Autumn Blaze'** maple (*Acer x freemanii*), a hybrid between the red maple and a tree that is often thought of as undesirable, the **silver maple**. It combines the best attributes of both parents: the tidy, oval outline and exceptional fall color of the red maple with the attractive, deeply lobed leaves and fast growth rate of the silver maple.

Sugar Maple

Another outstanding choice for the landscape, the native **sugar maple** is the tree that lights up hardwood forests east of the Mississippi in autumn with its stunning display of brilliant, golden orange color. **'Green Mountain'** has leathery, dark green leaves that are resistant to heat scorch and golden yellow to orange-red fall color that can be spectacular. It grows well in the North, but it is also tolerant of the heat and humidity of the South.

Red maple **grows well in damp or wet areas** and is tolerant of clay soils. Red maple is medium-sized and useful as a shade tree on smaller lots. Sugar maple is large and broad-spreading, best suited to larger landscapes. **FULL SUN** for best fall color. **ZONES 4 TO 8.**

Plant This!

This is another of those entries in this book that is not aiming to steer you away from a certain plant, but will hopefully introduce you to some of the newest and most beautiful varieties of already-popular species. New plant introductions are constantly being made in the horticultural world and trees are no exception. Each year, many new varieties enter the market in hopes of being noticed by homeowners and recently the native **redbud** (*Cercis canadensis*) has seen a tremendous resurgence in popularity with the introduction of no fewer than twenty new selections with many more on the way. Long admired for its spectacular, early spring show of purplish pink blooms covering its bare stems, the redbud makes a perfect understory or small specimen tree for landscapes of any size.

Floating Clouds™ Redbud

If it's a lighter and brighter spot you need in the landscape, try the new **Floating Clouds™ redbud**. It's highly variegated green and white leaves will not scorch, even in full sun, and its light pink flowers in early spring are a welcome sign that winter's grip is loosening.

While all of the forms mentioned here are of the standard, upright growth habit, many weeping forms are also being introduced. Excellent as ornamental specimens and focal points for small gardens, varieties such as **'Ruby Falls'**, **'Whitewater'**, and **'Traveller'** should not be overlooked.

■ New selections of redbud provide **long seasons of landscape interest** with beautifully colored foliage, as well as flowers. Weeping forms make excellent ornamental focal points for smaller landscapes. Improved forms maintain leaf color throughout hot, humid summers without fading or scorching.
■ **FULL TO PART SUN.** ■ **ZONES 4 TO 9.**

Merlot™ Redbud

If you find the dark-leafed 'Forest Pansy' redbud attractive, then you will love **Merlot™**. When 'Forest Pansy' begins to fade in midsummer, its leaves turning an unattractive shade of bronze, **Merlot™** holds its glossy, near-black leaves with little fading or discoloration, lending its deep, dark color to the landscape throughout the summer and well into autumn. Like 'Forest Pansy', its spring blooms are a sumptuous shade of deep, purplish pink.

The Rising Sun™ Redbud

The newest redbud introductions have spectacular foliage color in addition to their beautiful spring blooms, which give the trees many months of beauty and interest in the landscape. One of the most dazzling is **The Rising Sun™ redbud**, introduced by Ray and Cindy Jackson of Jackson Nursery in Belvidere, Tennessee. With bright, golden yellow leaves and orange new growth, it continues its colorful show long after its early spring flowers have faded. Where many golden or variegated plants may scorch in summer's heat and humidity, the leaf color of **The Rising Sun™** actually intensifies as the summer goes on, continuing right up to leaf drop in late autumn.

Plant This!

River birch (*Betula nigra*) is one of the most popular landscape trees in the country. Not only is it beautiful with its broad, spreading crown and spectacular, peeling, papery bark in shades of white, cream, beige, and salmon, it is fast-growing and usually quite inexpensive as compared to other trees, making it a common choice for new homeowners. Unfortunately, little thought is given to the tree's ultimate size (a 70-foot tree doesn't belong by the front door) or several inherent problems. Its large and invasive root system spreads far and wide in search of water, including into the foundations of homes. Without enough water it quickly becomes messy, dropping twigs and leaves throughout the summer, making for constant cleanup of its debris.

American Yellowwood

The **American yellowwood** (*Cladrastis kentukea*) is a fine, medium-sized native tree with many positive attributes. It has excellent flowers, foliage, and bark; maintains a good rate of growth; and can be used either as a shade tree on smaller, urban lots or as a medium-sized ornamental on larger properties. Clusters of fragrant white flowers hang from the tree in mid-spring, and fall color is often a clear and lustrous yellow. Smooth bark mottled in shades of silvery gray adds winter interest to the landscape. Ultimately reaching 30 to 40 feet tall with a similar spread, it will not overwhelm the landscape, and its deep, noninvasive roots are less likely to invade foundations or cause problems for lawns or landscaping.

■ American yellowwood has **showy, fragrant white flowers** and is especially beneficial to honeybees. It is well suited to today's smaller landscapes, being of medium size and having a noninvasive root system. Yellowwood's **smooth, silvery gray bark is especially attractive in the winter** landscape. ■ **FULL SUN.** ■ **ZONES 4 TO 8.**

Black Gum

Another outstanding alternative to the river birch is the native **black gum** (*Nyssa sylvatica*). Of more modest size, it grows 35 to 45 feet tall with a similar spread, making it well suited to the landscape as a specimen tree or moderately sized shade tree. Its spectacular and consistent fall color is lustrous, deep red. Black gum has a tremendous range of hardiness, from Zones 3 to 9, making it one of the most adaptable native trees where climate is concerned. However, it is somewhat particular about pH, preferring neutral to acidic soil, and is not particularly well suited to regions where limestone bases create alkaline soil conditions.

■ Black gum may be intolerant of high pH soils, preferring acidic conditions and excellent drainage. **Exceptional red fall color** makes sourwood a favorite native ornamental tree. **Sourwood is well suited to today's smaller landscapes,** being of medium size and having a noninvasive root system. ■ **FULL SUN.** ■ **ZONES 5 TO 9.**

SIBERIAN ELM

Plant This!

Japanese Zelkova

Originally touted as the replacement for the American elm, which was quickly succumbing to Dutch elm disease, **Japanese zelkova** (*Zelkova serrata*) is perhaps not as elegant as the American elms of old, but makes a fine substitute both for the Siberian and Chinese elms in gardens where another alternative is needed. Zelkova is a handsome, upright tree in its youth, becoming more vase-shaped as it ages. Fast-growing when young, it may grow as much as 3 feet a year under ideal conditions. **'Green Vase'** and **'Village Green'** are both popular varieties, and a form known as **'Variegata'**, available through several collector's nurseries, has a beautiful white margin on each leaf.

Much confusion exists in the nursery trade between this plant, **Siberian elm** (*Ulmus pumila*), and one of its relatives, the Chinese or lacebark elm. Siberian elm is an undesirable species of little use, but it is unfortunately misidentified as its more desirable cousin, *Ulmus parvifolia*, the lacebark elm. The ultimate weed tree, Siberian elm was once widely planted and now sprouts up everywhere, from highly manicured yards to abandoned lots and seemingly everywhere in between. Regrettably, its misidentification means that it is still grown and sold by a considerable number of nursery workers who simply don't know the difference. Its one redeeming quality is that it is quite resistant to Dutch elm disease and has been useful in creating disease-resistant hybrids.

■ Zelkova is an **adaptable and handsome** tree suitable to open yards where it has room to grow, or as a street tree. **Fall color can be showy** in shades of gold, orange, red, or purple. Zelkova is particularly good in the South, growing well into Zone 8.
■ **FULL SUN.** ■ **ZONES 5 TO 8.**

Lacebark Elm

Many horticulture professionals would argue that the **lacebark elm** (*Ulmus parvifolia*) is just as weedy and undesirable as its cousin, the Siberian elm. Admittedly, it does seed about with some abandon, especially in the garden, but the seedlings are small and easily removed and you're usually weeding in the spring anyway. Its propensity to produce viable seed aside, the **lacebark elm** does have a number of redeeming qualities. It is tough, durable, and will grow on almost any site, in any type of soil. The bark flakes off, sometimes in rather large sections, giving a beautifully patterned and mottled look to the tree trunk and larger limbs. Most important, perhaps, is the fact that it seems nearly impervious to Dutch elm disease. For additional color in the landscape, consider the cultivar **'Golden Rey'** with golden yellow leaves in spring, summer, and fall.

■ Lacebark elm is an excellent choice where a **tough, durable tree** is needed to thrive in a difficult situation. Lacebark elm has smooth, silvery gray bark that flakes and peels to reveal attractive cinnamon and tan new bark underneath. ■ **FULL SUN TO PART SUN.** ■ **ZONES 4 TO 9.**

Plant This!

Like the ginkgo and many other ornamental and shade trees, it isn't the **sweetgum** tree (*Liquidambar styraciflua*) itself that is the problem. It's the fruit! Spiky, spiny, hard round seedpods that drop from the sweetgum in late summer and autumn create an enormous mess in the yard. On hard surfaces such as sidewalks and driveways, where they will roll underfoot, they can even be quite dangerous. Fortunately, because many nurserymen and nurserywomen have spent years selecting a wide variety of useful and desirable forms of popular plants, there is almost always an answer to a problem tree. It is no different for the sweetgum.

Red Oak

If the thought of even a few spiky sweetgum pods gives you cause for concern, but you enjoy the thought of having nice fall color, **red oak** (*Quercus rubrum*) also may make a good substitute. While it is not seedless, its acorns are relative small and ultimately less messy than the large, ping-pong-ball-sized seeds of the sweetgum. Nearly identical in size and growth habit, the red oak also bears semiglossy, sharply pointed leaves, and while its fall color may not be as spectacular as the sweetgum, it can be a pleasantly bright shade of red in autumn. It is also one of the faster growing oaks, often averaging 2 feet per year in its youth, making a nice specimen in less than 10 years and an impressive shade tree as it ages.

■ Red oak is a valuable and **fast-growing substitute** of similar size to sweetgum. Autumn color is not as showy as sweetgum, but can be a pleasing red in most years. Fast-growing in its youth, red oak makes a nice tree in a few years' time.
■ **FULL SUN.** ■ **ZONES 4 TO 8.**

'Rotundiloba' Sweetgum

Sweetgum is one of the most desirable native trees for its strong, sturdy structure; fast rate of growth; and exceptional fall color in shades of gold, orange, and deep red. In fact, they can be so spectacular in autumn that they almost look as if they're on fire. Their only drawback, really, is the copious quantity of seedpods they produce and the fact that those seedpods are hard and woody and aren't going to disappear on their own once they fall to the ground. **'Rotundiloba'** is a form that is known to produce fewer fruits than most other varieties. Some sources even call it fruitless, which isn't quite accurate, but close. Its unique leaves have rounded tips instead of the traditional, sharply pointed ones, giving it a slightly different appearance in the landscape.

■ Sweetgums are deeply rooted trees whose roots **rarely cause problems for building foundations** or the buckling of sidewalks and driveways. "Fruitless" forms of sweetgum may still bear some seedpods, but in much less quantity than the standard forms. ■ **FULL SUN.** ■ **ZONES 5 TO 9.**

CHAPTER 5

Shrubs

Shrubs form the backbone of most of our landscapes and gardens. They are what we see at eye level as we look around us, screening undesirable views, anchoring building foundations, and adding beauty to our surroundings with their form, texture, and color. Shrubs provide sources of food and shelter for many beneficial insects, birds, and animals, contributing to lively and healthy ecosystems in our yards and gardens.

For practical purposes, shrubs can be divided into two main categories: those that are grown for their ornamental value, whether its flowers, berries, bark, or architectural form and those that, while still beautiful, may be more utilitarian in nature. The latter are those we often use for marking property boundaries, screening unsightly views, or creating privacy between the neighbors and us. The good news is that many shrubs cross over those categories and we can have shrubs that are functional, as well as beautiful, throughout our yards and gardens.

Each year researchers, hybridizers, and nurserymen around the world offer the latest in improved and more useful shrubs to gardeners everywhere. New varieties of hydrangeas are entering the marketplace at breakneck pace. How do you know which ones to buy? Butterfly bushes have been added to the list of invasive exotic species in some states, but are they problems everywhere and are there varieties that will not reseed and invade native landscapes? What about the Knockout® rose and the rose rosette disease that seems to be plaguing that plant throughout the country? Could this be the downfall of what has arguably become the most popular flowering landscape plant of all time? Read on to find the answers to these questions and for suggestions on how to make the best shrub choices for your landscape.

Plant This!

Barberry (*Berberis* species and hybrids) has been a longtime favorite in landscapes across the country. Deciduous species—those that lose their leaves—frequently have brightly colored foliage that adds beauty and drama to the landscape from early spring until late autumn. Other species are evergreen with deep green, often glossy leaves in a variety of interesting shapes and sizes. Nearly all barberries are armed with sharp spines along their stems and occasionally, especially on the evergreen species, on their leaves. Many gardeners find the barberries' spiny nature undesirable to work around. That, coupled with the fact that barberry has been added to the ranks of invasive exotic species in some states, has led to gardeners questioning its continued use.

Coppertina™ Ninebark

If it's dramatic color you're looking for in your landscape, but you find barberry undesirable, consider the native **ninebark**, *Physocarpus opulifolius*. In the past decade, ninebark has been transformed from a coarse and gangly shrub with little ornamental value to a popular and highly desirable addition to most any landscape. Improvements in growth habit, leaf color, and size have brought it to the forefront when it comes to colorful, ornamental shrubs. If you like dark and dramatic foliage, varieties such as **Summer Wine™** and **Tiny Wine™** will be to your liking with their dark maroon leaves. **Coppertina™** more closely matches the color of traditional red barberry with its coppery orange leaves, and **'Nugget'** has bright gold foliage on a dense, compact plant.

■ Ninebark is an **excellent native alternative** to barberry in colder climates, with burgundy, copper, or gold foliage, depending on variety. Ninebark also adds winter interest to the landscape with its peeling bark that hangs in long shredded strips from the larger "trunks" of the shrub as it ages. ■ Ninebark will be most colorful in **FULL SUN.** ■ **ZONES 2 TO 7.**

Purple Pixie® Loropetalum

In Zone 7 and warmer (where barberries suffer anyway), consider some of the new compact and dwarf forms of *Loropetalum chinense*, **Chinese fringe flower**. What was once a leggy and unkempt shrub best suited to the woodland understory has, through modern day breeding and selection, become a front and center member of landscapes where winters are warm enough for them to survive. Exceptional forms such as **Purple Diamond®** and **Purple Pixie®** clothe themselves in leaves of deepest burgundy-purple, highlighted by raspberry pink flowers in early spring, the former growing to an attractive and manageable 5 feet tall and wide and the latter useful as a tall groundcover reaching only 2 feet tall, but spreading 5 to 6 feet wide. In the colder reaches of its hardiness zones, *Loropetalum* may lose its leaves in mid- to late winter, but will quickly releaf when temperatures warm in spring.

■ Loropetalum offers similar texture and color to barberry with the added advantage of showy spring flowers. It thrives in milder regions throughout the country. ■ **FULL SUN** in the milder climates of the Pacific Northwest and Upper South, but is best in **PART SUN** in the Deep South. ■ **ZONES 7 TO 9.**

BIGLEAF HYDRANGEA

Plant This!

'Annabelle' Smooth Hydrangea

If its big blooms you love, few hydrangeas have bigger blooms than *Hydrangea arborescens* **'Annabelle'**. A sterile selection of a species native to the southeastern United States, **'Annabelle'** blooms in early summer with its enormous trusses of creamy white blooms lighting up the summer landscape. Some gardeners dislike 'Annabelle' for its propensity to flop. If that's the case, try the new introductions **'Ryan Gainey'**, with slightly smaller blooms that don't weigh the plant down, or **Incrediball™**, whose enormous flowers are held perfectly upright on the sturdiest of stems.

Gardeners everywhere fall in love with images of robust, blue- or pink-flowering **hydrangeas** (*Hydrangea macrophylla*) that grace the pages of gardening books and magazines around the world. Often, those photos were taken on just the right day, at just the right moment for the plants to look their very best. The reality, when trying to grow them at home, is often not as sweet. Plants struggle to compete for water with the roots of nearby trees. Late frosts nip buds and destroy flowers for the season, and in colder climates, harsh winters may kill stems to the ground, delaying future flowering for years. Fear not! New introductions are being made each year that can help even beginning home gardeners grow hydrangeas with much greater success.

■ Hydrangeas often need more sun than gardeners realize. Even in the South, most need at least a half day of sun. Hydrangeas naturally wilt when the sun is on them to prevent water loss. If they perk back up when the sun goes down, they don't need water. ■ **HALF-DAY TO FULL SUN.** ■ **ZONES 5 TO 9.**

'Blue Billow' Lacecap Hydrangea

An often-overlooked species, *Hydrangea serrata* has much to offer gardeners everywhere. While its blooms are the more delicate lace caps and not the robust, full-form "mops" of its cousin, its flower power is every bit as good; the show it puts on when well grown is nothing short of spectacular. Combined with the fact that it is much more forgiving and easier to grow, gardeners should keep it firmly in mind when choosing hydrangeas for their gardens. **'Blue Billow'** and **'Bluebird'** are particularly good forms.

Endless Summer

For those who insist on growing the traditional mop-head hydrangeas, many new options now exist with plants that are more cold hardy and have the ability to flower on their new growth, even if they do get caught in a late spring frost. **Endless Summer**™ was the plant that led the way in that respect, and with each new gardening season it seems that more and more plants enter the market. Time will tell which are truly the best, but it seems the options are nearly endless.

BURNING BUSH

Plant This!

The nearly indestructible nature and fiery red fall color of **burning bush** (*Euonymus alatus*) have made it a top choice for homeowners when they are choosing plants for their landscapes or gardens. Its tidy growth habit and adaptability to shearing have also made it popular for screens and hedges. Its blooms are insignificant, and its seedpods, even though they turn red, are small and rarely showy. However, they produce a great quantity of seed, which, in some locations, germinates with great reliability. This has turned the burning bush from a thing of great beauty and desire into an escapee into woodlands and natural areas, where it can quickly become a nuisance.

Doublefile Viburnum

One of the most elegant of all flowering shrubs the **doublefile viburnum**, *Viburnum plicatum* var. *tomentosum*, is also one of the most useful shrubs for the landscape. Most commonly, it is **'Shasta'** that will be seen at your local nursery or garden center, and it is, perhaps, the finest. Understand that doublefile viburnums need some elbow room, as they spread about twice as wide as they are tall. **'Shasta'** comes in at about 6 feet tall, but with a 10- to 12-foot spread, its horizontal branches sweeping the ground and completely laden with pure white blooms for several weeks in mid-spring. **'Mariesii'**, an older form, remains popular as well and puts on a similar show. Fall color, while not as brilliant red as the burning bush, is often a deep plum highlighted with orange and yellow. Not bad at all!

■ Doublefile viburnum prefers rich, evenly moist soil. Doublefile viburnum's large size makes it best suited to larger landscapes and gardens. If you plant more than one variety of doublefile viburnum, you may be rewarded with branches full of red berries in autumn. ■ **FULL TO PART SUN.** ■ **ZONES 5 TO 8.**

'Henry's Garnet' Virginia Sweetspire

'Henry's Garnet' Virginia sweetspire, *Itea virginica*, is a more than acceptable substitute for burning bush for a variety of reasons. It is native, so no worries about it escaping into woodlands or natural areas. It is much smaller growing and easier to adapt to today's landscapes, reaching a compact 4 feet high with a 5- to 6-foot spread. Finally, 'Henry's Garnet' provides multiple seasons of interest in the garden. Fragrant white flowers appear between May and July, depending on what region of the country you garden in (earlier in the South and later in the North). Its fall color, a stunning shade of deep, garnet red is every bit as beautiful as the best burning bush. It is native to damp areas, making it useful in today's heavily irrigated landscapes, or in wet areas where other shrubs may struggle.

■ Virginia sweetspire, a native alternative to burning bush, is well suited to today's smaller landscapes. A moisture-loving shrub, it is **particularly useful in drainage areas or in low spots that retain water.** ■ **FULL SUN TO PART SHADE.** ■ **ZONES 5 TO 9.**

BUTTERFLY BUSH

Plant This!

Popular since its introduction to gardens in the late 1800s, **butterfly bush** (*Buddleia davidii*) is known for its extremely showy, fragrant flowers borne in long panicles throughout the summer. It was a favorite of famed English garden designers such as Gertrude Jekyll, who used it frequently in both informal cottage gardens and to loosen up the tight formality of more structured beds and borders. Attractive to a wide range of butterflies and beneficial pollinators, butterfly bush was embraced by American gardeners too, but in recent years its propensity to reseed has placed it on the "naughty" list in several states, and gardeners have begun searching for alternatives.

'Blue Chip' Butterfly Bush

The truth of the matter is, few other shrubs resemble the butterfly bush or can offer its spectacular display of blooms. Thankfully, a handful of plant breeders have been working on producing cultivars that are sterile or nearly so, and even in states such as Oregon, where butterfly bush is on the noxious weed list, these non-threatening forms are approved for sale. One of the first was **'Blue Chip'** (*Buddleia*), a dwarf form growing only 3 feet by 3 feet at maturity and whose deep, lavender-blue blooms are produced nonstop from early summer until frost. 'Blue Chip' has been joined by **'Ice Chip'**, a white-flowering form, and **'Lilac Chip'**, in softest lilac, both dwarf and also producing little to no seed.

'Miss Ruby' Butterfly Bush

Two outstanding plants introduced by North Carolina State University through the J. C. Raulston Arboretum, **'Miss Molly'** and **'Miss Ruby'** are also sterile, posing no threat to the natural environment. 'Miss Ruby' appeared first, with flowers in a shocking shade of reddish pink and was the top pick in public voting at Great Britain's famed Wisley Gardens out of more than 100 cultivars being trialed from around the world. 'Miss Molly', a child of 'Miss Ruby', came along shortly after and is much closer to the true red butterfly bush that gardeners have longed for. At only 5 feet tall and wide, 'Miss Ruby' is sized to fit nearly any garden.

Recently, the **Flutterby™ Series** also began appearing in garden centers around the country. Broken down further into dwarf and standard-sized forms, the series' most valuable contribution is the expansion of the color range of butterfly bush into the peach, coral, and tangerine spectrum with varieties such as **Flutterby Grande™ Tangerine Dream** and **Flutterby Grande™ Peach Cobbler**.

■ All varieties recommended here are considered sterile, allowing gardeners to grow butterfly bush without threatening nearby native habitats. Sterile forms will flower nearly nonstop and deadheading is only necessary to keep the plants looking tidy. **Regular water and fertilizer ensure profuse flowering.** ■ **FULL SUN.** ■ **ZONES 5 TO 9.**

OLD-FASHIONED CAMELLIA

Plant This!

Camellias (*Camellia japonica*) have enjoyed an enduring stretch of popularity in gardens throughout the Deep South, but for decades—centuries, in fact—gardeners in zones colder than Zone 8 could only look longingly at images of perfectly sculpted blooms and hope they might feast their eyes on such perfection in the greenhouses of a nearby botanical garden or local conservatory. Slowly, after much painstaking work by a few enterprising hybridizers, the genes of some of the hardiest camellias from the coldest parts of their native habitats were introduced, and a group of cold-hardy, modern-day hybrids were born. Today, traditional winter and spring-blooming camellias can be grown outdoors in gardens as cold as Zone 6.

'April Remembered' Camellia

While cold-hardy camellias first became available in the mid- to late 1990s, most were fall-flowering hybrids with *Camella sasanqua*, and while they were, and continue to be, highly praised and widely grown, they did not offer the traditional, formal-looking blooms that most gardeners associated with *Camellia japonica* and its hybrids. The introduction of the **April Series** to the mainstream nursery market in the early 2000s (they had been available through a handful of camellia nurseries prior to then) changed all of that. Finally, gardeners colder than Zone 8 were able to grow the traditional winter and spring-blooming camellia and enjoy its exquisite blooms outside of a greenhouse or conservatory. **'April Remembered'**, with its semiformal, blush pink blooms, led the way with other varieties soon following. **'April Blush'**, **'April Snow'**, **'April Kiss'**, **'April Rose'**, and others round out the series.

'Korean Fire' Camellia

Grown from seed collected by plantsman Barry Yinger on a cold, windswept island off of the Korean coast in the early 1980s, *Camellia* **'Korean Fire'** has survived 28 degrees below zero on his Pennsylvania farm. Finally becoming widely available in the trade, it has single red flowers, highlighted by a tuft of bright gold stamens at their center, that appear from late winter through spring. Its blooms spread out over a period of about six weeks in most climates. While the plant is slow growing, it can become quite large over time and should be sited in the garden with that in mind.

Further breeding and selection means that new, cold-hardy varieties continue to enter the marketplace, and with the addition of several exceptionally hardy forms of the **tea camellia**, *Camellia sinensis*, it is possible that future camellias may be grown in even colder zones.

■ Best grown in morning sun with afternoon shade or in bright dappled shade under a high tree canopy. **Need good drainage to be successful.** Heavy clay soils should be thoroughly amended with organic matter. ■ **PART SUN TO PART SHADE.** ■ **ZONES 6 TO 9.**

Plant This!

At one time, an extremely popular landscape plant and still so in certain climates, the **firethorn** (*Pyracantha coccinea*) was widely grown for its breathtaking display of brilliant orange berries in autumn. Beloved by birds, it has been added to the list of invasive exotic species in some locations and in others has fallen out of favor for other reasons. Its unfriendly thorns make it difficult to place in the landscape, and in the South, lace bugs have become a persistent pest that leave the plants looking worse for wear by midway through the summer. Fireblight is a serious disease that can affect firethorn in all climates and various scab diseases may ruin the fruit before it colors up in fall.

Koreanspice Viburnum

Often, it is plants such as firethorn that produce copious quantities of berries that are also some of our most pernicious pests. When considering alternatives, then, you might have to give up one desirable characteristic, berries, for instance, for a more positive one like intoxicating fragrance. Few other shrubs offer more fragrance than some of the viburnums and **Koreanspice viburnum** (*Viburnum carlesii*) tops that list. In early spring, clusters of pink buds open to pure white blooms whose spicy fragrance can be smelled throughout the garden. It is the parent of two equally exceptional hybrids, the **fragrant viburnum** (*Viburnum x carlcephalum*) and **Judd viburnum**, (*Viburnum x juddii*), both equally as fragrant and desirable in the garden. In addition to their beautiful flowers and terrific fragrance, all will take on some shades of red and gold in autumn, though the intensity of their color may vary, depending on the year and the weather.

Linden Viburnum

When it comes to spectacular displays of autumn berries, few plants can rival a well-grown **linden viburnum**, *Viburnum dilatatum*. Over the years, many selections have been made from dwarf forms such as **'Catskill'**, topping out at 5 feet tall by 8 feet wide, to yellow-berried forms such as **'Xanthocarpum'** that shine in the autumn sun. Though it is an Asian plant, it is especially well behaved, and while it does form large quantities of berries, it seems not to reseed and cause problems for native habitats. Other equally attractive varieties include **'Iroquois'**, **'Mt. Airy'**, **'Catskill'**, and **'Oneida'**.

■ Linden viburnum will set the most berries when you plant more than one variety in close proximity to one another. **Berries will persist well into the winter until eaten by birds.** Fragrant viburnums offer a different, but just as desirable alternative with no concerns of them becoming invasive. ■ **FULL SUN TO PART SUN.** ■ **ZONES 4 TO 8.**

Plant This!

Not necessarily a bad plant, but certainly overplanted, **Japanese holly**, *Ilex crenata*, has garnered a bad reputation simply because people are tired of looking at it. It has become the ubiquitous evergreen foundation plant throughout its hardiness range because it is inexpensive and easy to replace if it dies. Even landscape professionals are guilty of just "sticking it in" anywhere they need a quick and easy fix. That said, it's not all bad. It isn't invasive, it's actually fairly low maintenance once established, and it does provide evergreen interest throughout the year. It's just boring, and in recent years it has become afflicted with a couple of root diseases that cause plants to die off randomly.

Boxwood

Boxwood (*Buxus* species) is perhaps no less common than Japanese holly, but with enormous number of varieties on the market its ornamental value cannot be questioned. There are plenty of dwarf forms, to be sure, which can be easily and immediately substituted for Japanese holly and be much longer-lived and just as easy to maintain. They also grow more uniformly. For gardeners in the North, selections such as *Buxus microphylla* var. *koreana*, the **Korean boxwood**, are some of the hardiest forms and will grow well into the Chicago area and other cold regions given some protection from desiccating winter winds. A number of hybrids between the Korean boxwood and the **common boxwood** also exist, the best of these being varieties such as **'Green Gem'**, **'Green Mountain'**, and perhaps the best of all, **'Green Velvet'**.

■ Boxwood was once a strictly Southern plant, but cold-hardy species and hybrids have made is to that **gardeners as far north as Chicago can now enjoy them.** Variegated forms of boxwoods such as 'Maculata' and 'Variegata' off a unique twist on the traditional green form. ■ **FULL SUN TO PART SHADE.** ■ **ZONES 5 TO 8.**

Gumpo Azalea

From Zone 6b and warmer, the **Gumpo azalea**, a group of hybrids represented by **'Gumpo White'**, **'Gumpo Pink'**, and **'Gumpo Rose'**, may be considered as replacements for the dwarfest forms of Japanese holly where border or edging plants are needed. These azaleas remain evergreen throughout the year and have the added benefit of putting on a spectacular floral show for about a month in late spring, after most other azalea varieties have finished. Other compact forms of azalea include the **Kurume hybrids**, with popular varieties such as **'Coral Bells'**, **'Hershey's Red'**, **'Hino Crimson'**, and many others offering spectacular displays of spring blooms. While azaleas are not as easy to grow as the Japanese hollies, where they are successful, they will be nothing short of show-stopping.

■ Azaleas are known, wherever they can be grown, for their spectacular spring floral displays. **Some new hybrids will also flower a second time,** usually in autumn. Azaleas need acidic soil and even moisture at their roots to reach their full potential. ■ **PART SUN TO PART SHADE.** ■ **ZONES 6 TO 9.**

Spirea (*Spiraea* x *bulmalda*) is another of those plants that has become overplanted to the point of nausea in nearly every part of the country because it is virtually indestructible, hardy from Zones 3 to 8, flowers repeatedly through the summer, and is reasonably low maintenance. That said, recent introductions have made the plant more palatable, taking away some of its negative attributes and replacing them with positive ones. Still, when it comes to flowering shrubs, there are a great many choices available and there is no need to be single-minded about them. If you insist on growing some form of spirea, at least look at some of the best, such as **'Goldflame'** or **'Limemound'**. Otherwise, here are some wonderful alternatives.

Plant This!

Dwarf Crape Myrtle

While there have been dwarf forms of **crape myrtle** around for many years, most were seed grown and were not uniform in their growth habits, flowering times, or colors. Slowly, advances in breeding were made, and new varieties were introduced. Now, gardeners and homeowners are blessed with a wide array of choices of crape myrtles of all shapes and sizes, but especially of new dwarf forms that make excellent landscape and garden subjects. From Zone 6 to 9, they make great substitutes for some more run-of-the-mill flowering shrubs. One of the first dwarf cultivars on the scene that is still popular today was **'Pocomoke'**, an attractive, lavender-flowered shrub that tops out at 3 feet by 3 feet and flowers from midsummer until fall. More recent introductions include the **Razzle Dazzle® Series**, made up of varieties such as **Cherry Dazzle®**, **Berry Dazzle®**, **Diamond Dazzle®**, and others. Many of these are exceptionally compact, topping out at less than 2 feet tall and wide. They flower from mid- to late summer, and several have red or burgundy tints to the leaves that add an extra layer of interest to the plant.

■ New selections of dwarf crape myrtle are disease resistant, have colorful foliage, and **bloom throughout the summer.** Crape myrtles are some of the most heat- and drought-tolerant shrubs. ■ **FULL SUN.** ■ **ZONES 6 TO 9.**

'Lilac Chip' Butterfly Bush

Already covered earlier in the chapter (see page 142), the new **dwarf butterfly bushes** such as **'Blue Chip'**, **'Lilac Chip'**, **'Ice Chip'**, and others also make excellent alternatives to the Japanese spirea. New cultivars are sterile, so there is no concern for them becoming invasive, and because they set no seed, they continue to flower throughout the growing season. Their only required maintenance is regular feeding and watering to keep them flowering profusely and occasional deadheading, not for seed removal, but to tidy up the plants.

■ For gardeners in Zones 5 and warmer, dwarf butterfly bush makes a good alternative, flowering throughout summer. **Regular water and fertilizer will ensure profuse flowering.**
■ **FULL SUN.** ■ **ZONES 5 TO 9.**

Plant This!

Popular for its fine-textured evergreen leaves, beautiful clusters of red berries in fall and winter, and the fact that once established it is nearly indestructible in the landscape, **nandina** (*Nandina domestica*) continues to be one of the most popular evergreens in Zones 6 to 9, where it is hardy. In recent years it has come under fire from native plant enthusiasts because it sets copious quantities of seed that are distributed far and wide by birds that relish its berries. It is a bigger problem in some regions than in others. A cautious eye should be kept on these plants and, depending on where you live, if it appears to be a problem, removal should be considered.

'Pink Frost' Anise Bush

Long thought to be a plant only for the Deep South, **anise bush**, *Illicium floridanum*, is making its way farther north and with good success. While almost no other plant has the same texture or growth habit as nandina, anise bush does make a good alternative that is both native and evergreen. Its broad leaves are almost rhododendronlike in appearance, and its maroon, fringy-petal blooms, while not terribly showy, are interesting when they appear in spring. **'Pink Frost'**, a recent introduction, is beautifully variegated, with each green leaf being margined in creamy white and adding to its year-round interest.

■ Florida anise bush is an attractive native alternative to nandina. Variegated forms of Florida anise bush add to the plant's beauty and year-round interest. Once established, Florida anise bush is **quite drought tolerant,** even recovering from a hard wilt once water is applied. ■ **PART SUN TO PART SHADE.** ■ **ZONES 6B TO 9.**

Winterberry Holly

If its nandina's red berries you love in your winter landscape, consider the native **winterberry holly**, *Ilex verticillata*, as an alternative. While it is not evergreen, the show it creates with stems full of brilliant red berries from late fall through midwinter is second to none. Male and female flowers are borne on separate plants, the females producing the berries, so keep in mind when purchasing that you need at least one male plant for every five females to get berries.

■ If berries are your goal, winterberry holly comes in a wide variety of shapes and forms and is **hardy to Zone 3.** Native to naturally damp or wet areas, **winterberry holly is useful in drainage areas, low places, and other locations where water stands for brief periods.** ■ SUN ■ ZONES 3 TO 9.

'Woodlanders Ruby' Anise Bush

While not available in every garden center, there are plenty of online sources for the anise bush called **'Woodlander's Ruby'**. This outstanding variety grows vigorously into a 6-foot by 6-foot shrub, and its evergreen leaves make a beautiful addition to the woodland understory. It has the added advantage of flowering repeatedly throughout the summer, with flushes of bloom appearing from midspring through late autumn in most years. Like all anise bush, the leaves are fragrant and spicy-scented when brushed against or crushed.

OAKLEAF HYDRANGEA

Plant This!

A longtime favorite, especially in gardens of the South and along the East Coast, **oakleaf hydrangea** (*Hydrangea quercifolia*) is one of the most beautiful native shrubs. Its spectacular show of blooms in early summer is the reason most homeowners choose it, but its bold foliage offers interest throughout the growing season, its ruby red fall color is rivaled by only a few other shrubs, and its peeling bark is attractive in winter, making it a truly useful shrub year-round. The only thing keeping more people from growing it is the fact that most of the varieties on the market can grow quite large, making it difficult to squeeze into the modern landscape. The few that are more compact often have less attractive flowers and growth habit.

'Munchkin' Oakleaf Hydrangea

The recent introduction of two new varieties by Dr. Sandy Reed of the USDA Research Center near McMinnville, Tennessee, will likely change the way that homeowners think of **oakleaf hydrangea** forever. Using the very best varieties on the market at the time, Dr. Reed began a fifteen-year quest to set a new standard in the world of oakleaf hydrangea. Her goal was to create compact plants with exceptional blooms that were easy to grow and care for, and she did not miss her mark. From more than 100,000 plants, the final group was narrowed down to fewer than 100 and of those, two were chosen for introduction with one or two more still under evaluation. The first to be introduced were **'Munchkin'** and **'Ruby Slippers'**, the former being a truly dwarf selection at only 2 feet tall by 3 feet wide and the latter, slightly larger at 4 feet by 4 feet with white flowers that turn ruby red as they age. Their smaller size and truly astounding floral display make them perfect for gardens of any and every size.

'Snowflake' Oakleaf Hydrangea

One of the least known, but perhaps the most beautiful oakleaf hydrangeas of all, is the variety **'Snowflake'**. Although unfortunately not well suited to the small garden because of its large size, any gardener who does have the room should not be without this hydrangea in their landscape. Enormous trusses of fully double, creamy white blooms cover the plant beginning in early summer, taking on a two-tone pink-and-white (or sometimes even tricolor—pink, white, and green) effect as they age.

■ An exceptional native shrub, more **compact selections make it suitable for landscapes of any size.** Shade tolerant, but best flowering will occur in at least a half day of sun or very bright dappled shade. Quite drought tolerant once established. ■ **PART SUN TO DAPPLED SHADE.** ■ **ZONES 5 TO 9.**

PANICLE HYDRANGEA

Plant This!

Little Lime™ Panicle Hydrangea

One of the first and most popular varieties of panicle hydrangea to take the gardening world by storm was **'Limelight'**, whose enormous flowers appeared in midsummer and retained their creamy chartreuse color throughout the life of the bloom, never turning white. The drawback was that the plant was enormous and many gardens simply couldn't accommodate its size. Recently, **Little Lime™**, a compact form with the same lime green blooms, was introduced, and now any garden, no matter the size, can benefit from its uniquely colored blossoms.

The rate at which new varieties of the **panicle hydrangea** (*Hydrangea paniculata*) are being introduced, even the professionals in the horticulture industry have a hard time keeping them all straight—or, quite frankly, knowing which ones perform the best. Panicle hydrangea is desirable for a number of reasons. It is easier to grow than many of its counterparts, especially the big, blue-flowering French hydrangeas, and it flowers later in the summer, extending hydrangea season well into July and August in many climates and sometimes later. Many varieties go through a dramatic change of color as the flowers age, turning from white at their peak to shades of pink as they age and sometimes to deepest red near the end.

QuickFire™ Panicle Hydrangea

Another recent introduction chosen for its compact habit and its large heads of white flowers that quickly change to pink and eventually as red as burning embers is **Quick Fire™**. Topping out at 5 feet tall by 5 feet wide, it is much easier to accommodate in today's landscapes than older varieties that grew nearly twice that. Its show begins in midsummer, and in most years the flowers will continue well on into autumn as the flowers age through various shades of pink and red.

As with the popular "mop-head" hydrangeas, new varieties are entering the market at an unheralded pace. Each season sees dwarf forms, earlier forms, later forms, more colorful forms, and nearly anything else the breeders can dream up. Part of their popularity stems from the fact that this entire group of hydrangeas flower on their new wood, so winter cold, late spring frosts, or accidental pruning at the wrong time of year mean you still get a summertime show, no matter what. The selections are truly endless.

■ Panicle hydrangea flowers on its new growth and its flowering will be unaffected by cold winters, late spring frosts, or improper pruning. Unlike many hydrangeas, panicle hydrangea prefers full sun, even in the South. Its **exceptional cold hardiness** allows northern gardeners to grow hydrangeas. ■ **FULL SUN.** ■ **ZONES 3 TO 8**.

THORNY ELAEAGNUS

Plant This!

Gardeners have a love-hate relationship with **thorny elaeagnus** (*Elaeagnus pungens*), sometimes referred to as autumn olive, though that is actually a different species. For those who love to arrange flowers, it is popular as a cut stem and lasts long in a vase. Wildlife gardeners like it because its dense growth makes excellent habitat for a wide variety of birds and small animals. Unfortunately, its enormous size and unruly habit mean that it is impossible to accommodate in most gardens. More important, it reproduces prolifically by means of berries that are eaten by the birds, which distribute the seed far and wide, causing it to be an invasive nuisance. It is now on the invasive exotic species list in a number of states.

'Edward Goucher' Abelia

An outstanding alternative to thorny elaeagnus, *Abelia* **'Edward Goucher'** is an outstanding hybrid with glossy green leaves, bronze new growth, and fragrant purple-pink flowers from late spring through late summer. Reaching 6 feet by 6 feet, it is half the size of elaeagnus, making it easier to accommodate in the landscape and it has none of elaeagnus' bad habits. Stems may be cut for flower arrangements, and its dense growth habit in the garden makes it a favorite place for birds to nest. Abelia's evergreen leaves make it a perfect choice for screening, hedges, and as a winter accent in the landscape. **'Canyon Creek' abelia**, a recent introduction, grows 5 feet by 5 feet and has brightly colored leaves in shades of copper and gold, taking on burgundy tints in winter. Fragrant white flowers appear in early summer.

■ Abelia is a perfect substitute for elaeagnus in warmer climates. Its flowering stems are useful for cutting and work well in summertime arrangement. **The dense shrubs make excellent cover for birds and wildlife.** ■ FULL TO PART SUN. ■ ZONES 6 TO 9.

'Lynwood Gold' Forsythia

An old-fashioned favorite that is often overlooked in favor of newer introductions, **'Lynwood Gold' forsythia** still can't be beat when it comes to low-maintenance, easy-care shrubs. Its spectacular floral show of golden yellow flowers signals the beginning of spring. Long stems make it perfect for cutting, and its dense growth is just the thing for nesting birds and as cover for other wildlife. It is also well suited to hedging and screening because its dense growth habit means that it continues to provide privacy even though it drops its leaves in winter. Newer forsythia introductions provide smaller-growing options such as **Show Off**® and **Golilocks**™, making the forsythia a good choice for even the smallest gardens.

■ Forsythia works well in colder climates instead of elaeagnus. Its early spring blooms **make excellent and long-lasting cut flowers** and its dense growth habit make it a haven for a variety of birds and small animals. ■ **FULL TO PART SUN.** ■ **ZONES 4 TO 9.**

CHAPTER 6

Vines & Groundcovers

Climbing to the tops of trellises and trees, attaching themselves to walls, or latching on to handrails and downspouts in an attempt to reach for the sky, vines are an important layer of the garden that many gardeners choose to ignore once they've thought about them and often don't consider in the first place. All of that climbing is just too much trouble. How do you maintain it once it reaches the top of the chimney or, worse, the top of a tree? First, you make good choices to begin with, which is what this chapter aims to help you do, steering you away from the most aggressive and egregious characters and recommending some less athletic varieties for you to consider. Let's see if we can avoid some of the headaches and shine the spotlight on some of the very best.

Groundcovers are not much different, really. They spread horizontally instead of vertically, but beyond that, they're sort of like a vine on the ground. In some cases, that might be exactly what they are! Wintercreeper euonymus, for example, will grow perfectly well as a groundcover, which is its most common use, but let it get near a tree for just one minute—okay, maybe a little more than *one* minute, but not much—and it goes sprinting straight up the trunk to do an aerial ballet among the branches. Even groundcovers that stay firmly planted on terra firma can be a real problem, invading garden beds, choking out desirable plants, and making life generally miserable for garden and gardener alike. With the suggestions that follow, perhaps you'll be able to avoid some of the pitfalls of planting some of nature's most aggressive plants.

Plant This!

One of the most pernicious pests of the garden, **bishop's weed**, *Aegopodium podagraria* 'Variegata', will run over, under, around, and through any plant that gets in its way. While it is delicate in appearance, it is far from it in athleticism. And while it is unlikely to choke out too many of your other plants, its roots will invade theirs, and every time you dig and divide, you will move the bishop's weed along with whatever you're transplanting—even worse if you're sharing plants with friends! I'd sooner be given a cold, I think. You can get over that in a few days' time. Nurserymen and nurserywomen who are still selling this plant need a stern talking to, at least.

Shuttleworth Ginger

To cover gingers in any depth is not possible here, but a few worthwhile native species make wonderful substitutes to some of our nonnative aggressors. **Shuttleworth ginger**, *Asarum shuttleworthii*, is one of those. Native to the southeastern United States, it has heart-shaped, evergreen leaves that are often mottled in varying degrees of silver. Hardy to Zone 5, it grows well farther north, even though it is a southern native. A particularly nice form, **'Callaway'**, has small, heart-shaped leaves that are very heavily marked in silver, and while not common in the trade, it can be found through several mail-order nurseries online. Our more common native species, **Canadian ginger**, *Asarum canadense*, is deciduous but just as valuable as a groundcover in the woodland garden. Emerging in early spring, it is in full leaf from late March through October, and even when it is dormant in winter, its thick rhizomes that creep just below the soil surface help to prevent erosion, which is part of any good groundcover's job.

■ Native gingers come in evergreen and deciduous forms. ■ **PART SHADE TO SHADE.** Most evergreen species are slightly less hardy, usually **ZONES 6 TO 8**, unless otherwise stated. ■ *Asarum canadense*, the Canadian ginger, is hardy to **ZONE 3** and as warm as **ZONE 7**, making it highly useful in northern gardens.

Strawberry Begonia

Going by the common names **strawberry begonia**, or **strawberry geranium**, of which it is neither, *Saxifraga stolonifera*, from Zone 6 and warmer, makes a colorful alternative to more ill-behaved groundcovers such as bishop's weed. Its olive-green leaves are delicately striped in silver, and the undersides of the leaves are red. Several variegated forms now exist as well, adding even more beauty at ground level with leaves margined in white or shades of gold and marbled randomly with silver markings. Where it is hardy, it is at least semievergreen and in warmer zones completely evergreen, making it useful in winter as well as summer. It needs part shade to be at its best, but is surprisingly drought tolerant and resilient, once established.

■ Strawberry begonia is a **terrific groundcover** and is perfect for tucking into crevices in rock walls and between paving stones. Variegated forms add even more interest to the garden with their brightly colored leaves. ■ **PART SUN TO SHADE.** ■ **ZONES 6 TO 9.**

INSTEAD OF
BLACK-EYED SUSAN VINE

Plant This!

Moonvine

If you have the room for a larger growing vine, consider of the most dramatic and brilliant of all annual vines, the **moonvine**, *Ipomoea alba*. Not for a tiny courtyard garden unless you have plenty of space to support it, the moonvine can wind its way 15 to 20 feet or more up a support in a single season. Planted from seed sown directly in the ground after the soil is warm to the touch, moonvine will grow rapidly until it reaches the top of whatever structure it is growing on. Then it will begin to branch and vine and branch some more, completely consuming whatever it is planted on or near. Soon after, in mid- to late summer, it will open its first pure white flowers more than 6 inches across. The unusual thing is that instead of flowering in the early morning like its cousin, the morning glory, the moonvine opens its blooms at dusk and does it so quickly that you can actually watch them open.

■ Moonvine seed is **sowed directly outdoors** where you want it to grow once the soil is warm to the touch. It is a large growing vine and needs a sturdy trellis or fence on which to climb. **Pure white, 6-inch blooms open dramatically at dusk.** ■ **FULL SUN.** ■ **ANNUAL.**

Black-eyed Susan vine (*Thunbergia alata*) is an annual vine that was popular with my grandmother's—and even my great grandmother's—generations. Eventually, its popularity waned due to its somewhat finicky temperament and often shy flowering. Recent breakthroughs in breeding have lead to a resurgence in the black-eyed Susan vine's popularity, so here we'll take a look at a few of the new varieties—some in subtler shades—that have made it once again an attractive and sought-after addition to trellises, arbors, and containers in almost every gardening zone, as well as one outstanding alternative for those of you who have an aversion to the bright gold, orange, or sunset shades of the black-eyed Susan vine's blooms.

'Spanish Eyes' Black-Eyed Susan Vine

For decades, black-eyed Susan vine was only available from seed, which you had to start yourself on the kitchen windowsill to get them growing before it was time to plant outdoors. The color range was limited to yellow with a black eye, orange with a black eye, and white with a black eye, all of which were beautiful, but didn't offer much in the way of uniqueness. Recent selections offer a new range of color, which include, but are not limited to, **'Spanish Eyes'**, a mix of reddish colored sunset shades; **'Blushing Susie'**, with a soft yellow flower heavily blushed in red; **'Arizona Red'**, as close to solid red as they come; and the **Sunny™ Series**, whose colors include the typical orange and golden yellow, but also **'Lemon Star'**, a sunny lemon yellow.

■ Black-eyed Susan vine can be used either as a **climbing vine or as a cascading filler** for dramatic pots and containers. Black-eyed Susan vine grows best in rich soil and with regular water and fertilizer to keep it growing and blooming all summer. ■ **FULL SUN TO PART SUN.** ■ **ANNUAL.**

CHAMELEON PLANT

Plant This!

Lured by its exquisitely colored leaves of deep green splashed randomly with shades of gold, pink, and red, unsuspecting homeowners buy **chameleon plant** (*Houttuynia cordata*) thinking of all the beautiful combinations its colorful foliage will make with other garden residents. But do you remember the movie *Gremlins*? Do you remember what happened when you added water or, worse, fed them? To refresh your memory, they quickly morphed from cute and cuddly into sly, cunning, and devastating creatures. So, too, the chameleon plant! I cannot think of enough ways to tell you to avoid this plant at all costs except, maybe, in a container with no holes sitting in the middle of a water garden with no soil in sight. Even then, I question its use.

Chinese Wild Ginger

Though not quite as colorful as the chameleon plant, the **Chinese wild ginger** (*Asarum splendens*) does have heart-shaped, dark green leaves mottled with varying degrees of lighter green and shiny silver, making it more than bright enough to attract attention on the floor of the woodland garden or on a shady bank, mixing and mingling with hostas, ferns, and Lenten roses. Where it's happy, it will spread fairly quickly through the shady garden, forming an evergreen groundcover under and around neighboring plants. Only the smallest and most delicate of woodland plants need worry about it running over them, but you might keep an eye on those. A tough and resilient plant, Chinese ginger will perform best in good soil with adequate moisture, but it is surprisingly drought tolerant once it is fully established. This is but one species of many, and most of them make highly desirable garden plants.

■ There are both clumping and spreading forms of Chinese wild ginger. Many make tidy clumps or small colonies, **perfect for evergreen accents in smaller gardens.** Flowers appear at ground level in early to mid-spring and are pollinated by insects crawling in and out. ■ **PART SHADE TO SHADE.** ■ **ZONES 6 TO 8.**

Variegated Solomon's Seal

Where variegated leaves are desired to brighten up a shady spot where the chameleon plant might otherwise have made its home, look no further than the **variegated Solomon's seal**, *Polygonatum odoratum* 'Variegatum'. If you were considering chameleon plant, a deciduous groundcover itself, then the Solomon's seals winter dormancy should not be a factor, and its infinitely better behavior should already have you sold on its usefulness. Good behavior combined with stunningly variegated green and white leaves make it the perfect resident of the shade garden. Spreading at a medium rate, once established, it can form large colonies over time, but I know few gardeners who wish they had less of it. Newer and more unusual varieties, including **'Fireworks'**, **'Double Stuff'**, **'Doublewide'**, and others have recently caught the attention of even the most discerning plant collectors.

▪ Large colonies of Solomon's seal are **easily divided in autumn to increase the size of existing colonies** or establish new ones. New introductions continue to expand the range of sizes, colors, and habits of Solomon's seals, making them collectors' favorites. ▪ **PART SUN TO SHADE.** ▪ **ZONES 3 TO 8,** depending on species.

ENGLISH IVY

Plant This!

On the list of plants that you "can't live with, but can't live without," **English ivy** (*Hedera helix*) is likely at the very top. An indispensible "filler" for outdoor pots and planter boxes, English ivy's amazing array of leaf shapes and colors add dimension and drama to container plantings everywhere. As a groundcover, it was the go-to plant for dry shade for decades, but like many vines that double as groundcovers, the minute it reaches a tree, it heads skyward. In a matter of a few years, it can completely engulf even the largest shade trees, its immense weight breaks limbs from weaker trees, and its strangling stems squeeze the life out of those that remain.

Evergreen Solomon's Seal

Little known or grown until about a decade ago, **evergreen Solomon's seal** (*Disporopsis pernyi*) is a fairly recent introduction from China that is now beginning to appear with some regularity in nurseries and garden centers around the country. It spreads slowly, so when used as a groundcover it should be planted about 2 feet apart so that plants will cover their space in a reasonable amount of time. Because of its slow spread, it makes a perfectly behaved evergreen groundcover. White, bell-shaped flowers appear on the new growth in early spring. Hardy from Zones 6 to 9, it may prove even hardier, as it has the ability to become deciduous in colder climates, resprouting from its underground rhizomes in spring.

■ Evergreen Solomon's seal **spreads slowly by underground rhizomes** and may be deciduous in colder climates, but will resprout vigorously in spring. Small, white, bell-like flowers appear in spring. Prefers deep, woodland soils that are rich in leaf litter and other organic matter. ■ **PART SHADE TO SHADE.** ■ **ZONES 6 TO 9.**

Lenten Rose

While not typically thought of as a groundcover, since it doesn't spread by the traditional means of vines or runners, the **Lenten rose** (*Helleborus* x *hybridus*) does make an excellent groundcover for shady, dry areas of woodland garden from Zones 5 to 8. Simply start by planting as many plants as you can afford to buy and plant them about 2 feet apart. In a couple of years' time, plants will have grown large enough to touch, covering the ground throughout the year with their evergreen leaves. Allow the plants to go to seed after they finish flowering each spring and soon you will have large colonies establishing themselves across the woodland floor. Many plants that are not typically thought of as "groundcovers" may be used in this way simply by planting them in masses large enough to cover the ground effectively. Evergreen plants such as the Lenten rose are especially well suited to this use. *Helleborus niger*, the **Christmas rose**, is even hardier, surviving into Zone 4.

■ Many evergreen perennials, such as Lenten rose, make excellent groundcovers when planted so that the plants will touch when they have reached their mature size. Lenten rose **will reseed to form spectacular colonies** over time. ■ **PART SUN FARTHER NORTH TO FULL SHADE IN THE SOUTH.** ■ **ZONES 5 TO 8.**

Japanese honeysuckle vine, *Lonicera japonica*, is another on the long list of plants that many gardeners have a love-hate relationship with. When it comes to fragrance, there are few other plants that can compete. Its sweet scent hanging in the heavy evening air of early summer is truly intoxicating and can seemingly transport the recipient of its heady aroma to an almost otherworldly place. On certain nights, you can almost taste it. The reality, however, is that Japanese honeysuckle vine is a destructive and harmful weed that has overtaken many a forest floor and fence row east of the Rocky Mountains, completely choking out any plant that gets in its way. To that end, it must be recommended against in the garden.

Plant This!

Carolina Jessamine

Flowering early in the season, but just as showy and pleasantly fragrant, is **Carolina jessamine**, *Gelsemium sempervirens*. Native to the southeastern United States, it is hardier than one might suspect, growing easily into the colder regions of Zone 6. While it can grow quite large over time, it is easily managed, and its delicate, twining stems rarely pose a threat to structures, nearby buildings, or even the trees it is found climbing where it grows wild. Bright, golden yellow, bell-shaped blooms appear in late winter and early spring, sometimes as early as February, and can be impressive when the vine is at its peak of bloom. The cheerful color is always welcome on the cold, gray days that seem to abound as spring tries to loosen winter's grip. Carolina jessamine is highly adaptable, growing in full to part shade and on sandy and clay soils alike. In the garden, given good soil, regular water, and occasional feeding, it will grow into a dense and beautiful evergreen vine that will be most impressive when in bloom.

■ Carolina jessamine is **highly adaptable,** tolerating a wide range of soil types and wet areas to dry. It is completely evergreen and flowers in late winter and early spring. Best performance is in rich, moist soil. ■ **FULL TO PART SUN.** ■ **ZONES 6 TO 9.**

Hyacinth Bean

If you don't mind an annual vine, give the purple-flowered, purple-podded **hyacinth bean**, *Dolichos lablab*, a try. Seed can be sown directly in the ground outdoors when the soil feels warm to the touch. Simply plant the seeds about 1 inch deep at the base of the structure where you want the vine to grow. Attach a string or two to help guide young shoots in the direction you want them to grow, and in no time, you'll have a robust vine covering whatever you've chosen to grow it on. Flowering begins in early to midsummer, and the royal purple pods that follow the blooms will hold their color until late in the fall.

■ Hyacinth bean is an annual vine, but its summer display of light purple flowers followed by royal purple bean pods is **worth planting new seeds each spring.** Seed can be sown directly in the garden when soil is warm to the touch. ■ **FULL TO PART SUN.** ■ **ANNUAL.**

Plant This!

For groundcover in deep shade, few plants can rival **Japanese pachysandra** (*Pachysandra terminalis*) when it is perfectly grown. Spreading by short, underground stolons, it creeps its way just under the surface of the soil, forming a carpet of green shoots and leaves as it goes. Pachysandra is one of the few plants that will grow in the shade of and compete with the roots of the Southern magnolia. While there is some concern about it escaping into natural areas, it rarely sets seed in most climates, and seedlings are few and far between in most gardens. Because its underground stolons are short, there is little concern of it running off into the woods unless it is planted directly at their edge, and even then, it can be controlled. But planted in full sun or when stressed by drought and other environmental factors, Japanese pachysandra becomes susceptible to several blight and leafspot diseases that can range from disfiguring but survivable, to fatal.

Alleghany Spurge

If the fact that common pachysandra is not native still concerns you, consider the native pachysandra, the **Alleghany spurge**, *Pachysandra procumbens*. It is an excellent groundcover for difficult shady spots, forming a soft carpet of gray-green leaves. In winter, the leaves lay down on or close to the ground, taking on distinct burgundy tones often marked in lighter green or silver. Alleghany spurge is a clump-forming species, so in order for it to cover the ground it must be planted close enough for mature plants to fill in and touch—18 inches on center should be sufficient.

■ All three selections **thrive as groundcovers** in shady woodland gardens. Pachysandra is completely evergreen with a minimal floral display. Creeping phlox is semievergreen, but its spring floral display is outstanding. Alleghany spurge is a clumping form, so plants must be spaced to touch when mature if a groundcover effect is desired. ■ **SHADE.** ■ Alleghany spurge **ZONES 4 TO 9.** ■ Creeping phlox **ZONES 2 TO 8.** ■ Varigated pachysandra **ZONES 4 TO 8.**

Creeping Phlox

Another native species that makes an outstanding substitute for pachysandra, *Phlox stolonifera* shares its common name, **creeping phlox**, with another groundcover phlox covered in a previous entry in this chapter. In this case, however, *Phlox stolonifera* bears small, flat leaves rather than the needlelike leaves of its cousin, and flowers are borne just slightly later in spring atop delicate wandlike stems to 12 inches tall. It's exceptionally tolerant of a wide range of climates.

Variegated Pachysandra

To add even more elegance to an already beautiful groundcover, consider the variegated form, ***Pachysandra terminalis* 'Variegata'**, to brighten up a dark, shady location in the garden. Each leaf is boldly margined in creamy white, taking pachysandra's already pleasing effect in the landscape to an entirely new level.

Paired with dark green hostas or the glossy, evergreen foliage of Lenten roses, the effect can be truly stunning. It also works very well with the soft, feathery foliage of an unusual shade-loving evergreen, the **Russian cypress**, *Microbiota decussata*, which forms a flat, ground-covering shrub.

Plant This!

Its extreme durability and truly "no maintenance" nature have made **liriope** (*Liriope spicata*), or monkeygrass, one of the most widely planted groundcovers and bed edgers anywhere. It is especially popular in the Southeast and along the East Coast, where it is used to fill almost any space, sun or shade, where little else will grow. It can be found in the finest shade gardens and the most desolate parking lots, growing without a care no matter where it's planted. There are two basic forms: one clumping, the other spreading. The clumping species, *Liriope muscari*, actually spreads, too, but at a very slow rate, while the other, *Liriope spicata*, spreads quickly by underground runners. Both set seed, and both, when planted near woodlands or natural areas, may invade those habitats.

Black Mondo Grass

Very closely related to liriope, but generally better behaved, are the mondo grasses. Represented in the trade almost exclusively by two species. **Dwarf mondo grass** (*Ophiopogon japonicus*) is the more common of the two and comes in an array of forms, some which are so small they look like Astroturf. Equally as popular, but very slow and expensive to produce, is **black mondo grass** (*Ophiopogon planiscapus* 'Nigrescens'). Highly sought after for its narrow, black leaves, it mingles well with small, lighter-colored hostas or with the brilliant chartreuse-gold groundcover called creeping Jenny. Neither is difficult to grow, but both are slower, less robust, and less tolerant of neglect than their close cousin, liriope.

■ Mondo grass prefers part sun in warmer regions, but will grow in full sun further north. It is touted as an **alternative for lawns,** but it is not fond of constant foot traffic. It is intolerant of car exhaust and a poor choice along driveways or parking areas.
■ **PART SUN TO FULL SUN.** ■ **ZONES 6 TO 8.**

Creeping Phlox

One of the most durable native groundcovers, **creeping phlox** (*Phlox subulata*) is a tough, drought-tolerant resident of roadside ditches and steep banks across the eastern half of North America. With an amazing native range from Zone 2 in the North to Zone 8 in the South, it will grow almost anywhere except in subtropical and warm coastal regions. Nearly anywhere else, it's fair game. It can be found growing at the summit of Mount Hood in Oregon and along the hot, humid roadsides of Tennessee. In early spring, it completely blankets itself in ¾-inch flowers in shades of light blue, purple, pink, and white. For about a month, its prickly evergreen leaves will be entirely obscured by the flowers. The remainder of the year it acts as a completely carefree, evergreen groundcover. **'Emerald Cushion Blue'** and **'Emerald Cushion Pink'** are two of the best selections and the most popular, for good reason. For white flowers, **'Snowflake'** is unsurpassed.

■ Creeping phlox (also called moss phlox) is an **exceptionally tough** native groundcover for difficult sites in full sun. In early spring, plants are blanketed with blooms of blue, lavender, pink, or white. Evergreen foliage is attractive year-round. ■ **FULL SUN.** ■ **ZONES 2 TO 8.**

Plant This!

Parfait® Series Mandevilla

One of the most exciting breakthroughs in breeding mandevilla was realized with the recent introduction of the **Parfait® Series**, whose fully double flowers resemble those of the finest roses or camellias. **Moonlight Parfait®**, a double-flowered white; **Pink Parfait®**, a double-flowered deep pink; and **Tango Twirl®**, a double-flowered pale pink, are the first of what are sure to become garden classics. Flowers are large, nearly 4 inches across, and extremely showy. Because of the energy it takes to produce such large and fully double blooms, regular fertilizing is a must throughout the growing season. A liquid "bloom booster" fertilizer can be applied every other week to keep plants producing new buds and blooms from spring until frost. Robust plants have the ability grow 8 to 10 feet in a single season if well watered and fed, making them perfect for covering larger trellises, arbors, and fences.

Finally, here is an entry that is not about finding a replacement for an aggressive, invasive garden thug. Instead, we'll just talk about pretty plants! **Mandevilla** (*Mandevilla* hybrids) have long been among gardeners' favorites for their large, brightly colored blooms in shades of bright pink, red, and sometimes white. A short time ago, new varieties began to find their way into greenhouses and garden centers around the country, and today, the choices seem nearly endless. There are single flowers, double flowers, large flowers, and small flowers. There are plants that grow into very large vines and plants that remain smaller and more compact. The exotic and seemingly endless array of flower forms and colors are unlike any that we have seen before on mandevilla.

'Red Riding Hood' Mandevilla

One of the earlier varieties to hit the market, **'Red Riding Hood'** is also one of the more compact selections of mandevilla, growing only 4 to 6 feet high, with smaller, glossy green leaves and smaller blooms only 2½ inches across, but produced in great quantity. Flowers are rich, deep pink and appear from spring through frost. Perfect for climbing up a small trellis or along a balcony rail, **'Red Riding Hood'** is also attractive to hummingbirds and other pollinators. Applying liquid fertilizer once a month throughout the growing season will promote the most vigorous growth and heaviest bloom. Other dwarf introductions include **Sun Parasol™ Pretty Pink** and **Sun Parasol™ Crimson**, whose growth habits and requirements are similar to 'Red Riding Hood'.

■ Mandevillas are **heavy feeders,** benefiting from monthly or even twice monthly applications of liquid fertilizer throughout the growing season. Full sun is required for the greatest flower production, though **plants will flower even in part sun.** Double-flowered forms need more sun than singles. ■ **PART SUN TO FULL SUN.** ■ **TROPICAL**; grown as an annual.

SWEET AUTUMN CLEMATIS

Another of the native vines that many gardeners have planted and then questioned their decision later, **sweet autumn clematis** (*Clematis paniculata*), while beautiful and highly fragrant when in bloom, can be an aggressive thug. This is especially true in smaller gardens that simply cannot accommodate its ultimate size, which may approach 20 to 30 feet or more, often in a single season. Where you have room, it is extremely effective and nothing short of show-stopping for the month in early autumn when it is in full bloom. Planted at the edge of the property where its fragrance can drift across the yard, it is a welcome sight and aroma, but for most gardens today, it simply grows too large.

Plant This!

'Amethyst Falls' Native Wisteria

Many gardeners, unless they were native plant enthusiasts, were unaware until the past decade that a **native wisteria** even existed. *Wisteria frutescens* **'Amethyst Falls'** is the plant that changed all that, offering a well-behaved native alternative not only for the aggressive and invasive species from China and Japan, but as a suitable alternative for other vines as well. Growing only 20 feet or so and in a much more delicate manner than its Asian counterparts, **'Amethyst Falls'** also has the added benefit of flowering repeatedly throughout the summer, producing one main floral display in late spring, followed by fewer, but consistent blooms throughout the summer. Another variety, **'Nivea'**, produces white flowers, but it is less widely grown and is more difficult to find in nurseries and garden centers, though several online sources make it available.

■ 'Amethyst Falls' wisteria flowers on new growth and **will bloom repeatedly** through the summer. Being native, there are no worries of it escaping and invading woodlands and natural areas. Less aggressive growth means **less maintenance and pruning required.** ■ FULL SUN. ■ ZONES 5 TO 9.

'H. F. Young' Hybrid Clematis

It would be remiss not to mention here that an astounding number of hybrid clematis exist, almost all of which are welcome members of any garden family. **'H. F. Young'** is one of the showiest with enormous blooms that reach at least 8 and sometimes 10 inches across in the most luscious shade of lavender-blue. Its early spring blooms stop people in their tracks when they are fully open, and it repeats at least once and occasionally twice if well watered and fed through the summer months. Other varieties too numerous to name bear flowers in shades from pure white through pinks, blues, purples, and deepest reds and in equally as many sizes and forms, from tiny blooms 1 inch across to 10-inch giants and from nodding blooms whose fat buds barely open to fully double forms that look almost like multi-petaled daisies when fully open.

■ Clematis prefer their tops in full sun, but their roots in the shade. **Perfect for tucking in between other plants** where they can scramble up a nearby shrub or trellis. Clematis come in a variety of heights, colors, and bloom sizes. ■ **FULL SUN TO PART SUN.** ■ **ZONES 4 TO 9,** depending on variety.

Spanish Flag

Native, but in this case one of those plants that, when not treated with a heavy hand, can become a garden thug in no time is **trumpet vine**. *Campsis radicans* is rampant and clinging, with rootlike holdfasts that sprout from its woody stems and cement themselves to anything that stays in one place for too long. When it reaches the top of its support, it will simply begin twisting around itself like a green tornado, forming a massive, bulbous head that reaches skyward. As rambunctious a grower as it is, its flowers are undeniably beautiful and attract hummingbirds and other pollinators for miles around. In a garden of size enough to accommodate it, it can be a blessing. Elsewhere, it may well be a curse.

If it's the orangey red color of the trumpet vine you love, perhaps you'll consider a beautiful annual vine to take its place. **Spanish flag** or **firecracker vine** (*Mina lobata*) is easily grown from seed in spring and with the heat of summer will quickly grow 6 to 8 feet or more. Beginning in late summer and continuing until frost, deep red flower buds fade to yellow and eventually creamy white as the flowers open in succession up the stem. With 50 to 100 clusters of blooms open at once on large, well-grown vines, they are nothing short of traffic-stopping.

■ Spanish flag and other **annual vines give you a longer season of color** compared to most perennial vines, whose floral displays are often brief. Annual vines give you the chance to change your color scheme from year to year. Spanish flag's tube-shaped, red flowers are **especially attractive to hummingbirds.** ■ FULL SUN. ■ ANNUAL.

Trumpet Honeysuckle

The very word "honeysuckle" strikes fear into many gardeners who immediately think of rampant vines or invasive shrubs that soon choke out anything in their path. *Lonicera sempervirens*, the native **trumpet honeysuckle**, is a well-behaved member of the family and is welcome in gardens of any size, as it is easily managed and will, mostly of its own accord, grow only to the size of whatever support it grows on. If it's on the mailbox, it will thoroughly, but politely cover it. Plant it on a larger structure and give it a little more soil at its roots and it will cover that, too, but never in an aggressive or undesirable way. In mid- to late spring, it glows in a luminous shade of coral-red as clusters of blooms engulf the plant from the previous year's growth. Blooms will continue to appear sporadically on new growth throughout the summer. Several yellow flowering cultivars have been selected, as well, the blue-green leaves forming the perfect backdrop for the clusters of sulfur yellow flowers.

■ Trumpet honeysuckle is a **noninvasive native honeysuckle** whose coral red blooms provide spring nectar for migrating hummingbirds and other pollinators. 'John Clayton' is a fine variety with yellow flowers instead of the typical coral red. ■ **FULL SUN TO PART SUN** for best flowering. ■ **HARDY ZONES 6 TO 9**.

Plant This!

There are two species of **vinca** that are commonly found on the market today: ***Vinca minor*** is a dry-shade-loving groundcover and ***Vinca major***, usually a variegated form that is being grown as annual for cascading over the sides pots and planters. Both, if left to their own devices, can be aggressive groundcovers, and if they're allowed to get firmly established in the garden or woodland, they can be a real nuisance to remove. The only real difference between the two is that ***Vinca major*** is larger in all aspects than ***Vinca minor***. Beyond that, they are quite the same, at least as far as daily appearances are concerned.

'Bath's Pink' Cheddar Pinks

Vinca, especially *Vinca minor*, is often incorrectly planted as a groundcover in sunny areas where it becomes stressed and eventually dies a slow and ugly death from a variety of stem and root rot diseases. This is a perfect example of picking the wrong plant for the wrong place instead of the other way around. Instead, for a hot, sunny area, consider the outstanding **'Bath's Pink' cheddar pinks**, *Dianthus gratianapolitanus* 'Bath's Pink'. Its silvery green, evergreen foliage grows only 4 inches tall, but plants can spread to nearly 4 feet wide in only two seasons. In early spring for about four to six weeks, the plants blanket themselves in light pink, extremely fragrant flowers with the scent of cloves. A tough and durable groundcover, cheddar pinks only ask for full sun and good drainage to thrive for many years.

■ 'Bath's Pink' cheddar pinks is an excellent perennial alternative to vinca in sunny areas where it will provide an outstanding floral display in spring and **year-round cover with silvery green foliage. It needs good drainage** and is not overly fond of constant irrigation. ■ **FULL SUN.** ■ **ZONES 3 TO 8.**

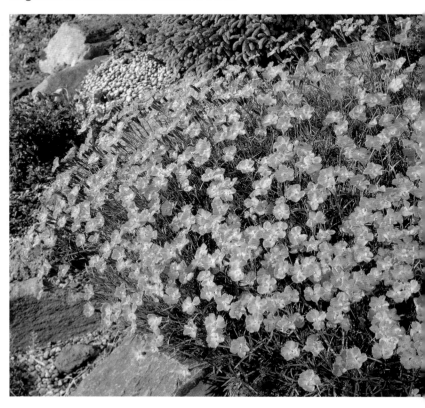

Lily-of-the-Valley

If it's a tough groundcover for the shady garden you're in need of, look no further than the **lily-of-the-valley**, *Convallaria majalis*. Known mostly for its delicate white spring blooms whose intoxicating fragrance can perfume a room, lily-of-the-valley is a much tougher plant than many gardeners might believe. One of the few plants that will thrive even under the dry shade of a cedar tree, it spreads quickly, once established, by way of underground stolons that increase the size

of the colony upon emergence each spring. If you're interested in looking beyond the typical green form, there are some dazzling variegated forms whose leaves add an extra element of color and interest to the garden. These include **'Vic Pawlowski's Gold'**, with green leaves heavily striped in creamy yellow; **'Cream da Mint'**, with green leaves banded by a gold margin; and **'Fernwood's Golden Slippers'**, an exceptionally vigorous form whose leaves are solid gold.

■ Lily-of-the-valley is a tough, reliable groundcover that **thrives in dry shade.** Variegated forms provide added contrast with nearby plants. White, bell-shaped, and sweetly fragrant blooms appear in spring. Perennial in nature, it **spreads slowly by underground runners,** forming larger colonies with each passing year. ■ SHADE. ■ ZONES 2 TO 7.

WINTERCREEPER

One of the very worst when it comes to exotic invaders from other parts of the world, **wintercreeper euonymus** (*Euonymus fortunei*) has creeped and crawled its way across woodland floors and up the tallest trees in forests across the eastern half of the United States. Once it gets a foothold, it is almost impossible to stop, except with much persistence and a fair amount of manual labor. Its leaves are thick and covered in a nearly impenetrable coat of wax that makes them impervious to even the strongest weed killers, which aren't good for you or the environment anyway. If it has invaded and climbed trees or other structures, you can kill it by cutting through its thick, woody stem and carefully painting the fresh cuts with a nonselective herbicide.

Barrenwort

Barrenwort (also called bishop's cap), *Epimedium* species and their hybrids, have become the recent darlings of the horticultural world. Once represented by about five cultivars that weren't seen with any regularity in garden centers, their popularity has exploded over the past decade, due primarily to the work of Darrell Probst, an intrepid plant explorer and nurseryman who introduced numerous species to cultivation from China and created a great many hybrids that are just now beginning to be distributed to gardeners. Barrenwort's popularity stems from the fact that most are easy to grow, many are evergreen or at least semievergreen, they flower profusely in spring, and, once established, many are exceptionally tolerant of dry shade, which is one of our most challenging growing conditions. Some are taller than others, but few exceed 18 inches in height when they are fully leafed out and many don't exceed 12 inches, making them perfect candidates for spreading in and around other woodland dwellers. While some are stoloniferous and will spread to form colonies, none are a threat to nearby plants.

■ Newer species and hybrids will need further testing to determine their full hardiness. Many **thrive in dry shade.** Different species may be evergreen, semievergreen, or deciduous, the latter being the most cold hardy of the group. ■ **SHADE.** ■ Many hardy to **ZONES 5 TO 6.**

European Ginger

If it's an evergreen groundcover for a shady location that you need, **European ginger** (*Asarum europaeum*) makes a fine choice. Growing only 6 inches tall and relegated to ground level (it can't climb), it will form dense colonies of shiny, evergreen leaves that remain attractive throughout the year. As new foliage emerges in spring, the old foliage simply lies down and withers away, requiring absolutely no maintenance or cleanup from you. The flowers are borne at ground level, usually under the new leaves of spring, and, while interesting, are far from showy. Especially good in northern climates, it is hardy to Zone 4 and is one of only a few evergreen groundcovers that will thrive in climates with especially cold winters.

■ European ginger is cold hardy to Zone 4, making it one of the most **cold-tolerant, noninvasive, evergreen groundcovers.** Prefers rich, loose, well-drained soil and is not well suited to heavy clay. ■ **PART SHADE TO SHADE.** ■ **ZONES 4 TO 7.**

YELLOW ARCHANGEL

Plant This!

Yellow archangel (*Lamiastrum galeobdolon*) doesn't sound like a plant that would be a problem in the garden or anywhere else for that matter, but names can be deceptive. A member of the mint family, it has the same ability to spread as some of the other poorly behaved members of that clan, and where it has escaped into the wild, it has quickly become a nuisance. It is on the watch list for invasive exotic species in several Mid-Atlantic states, as well as in the Midwest and on the West Coast. It can spread by aboveground runners, seed, and any piece of the root that is left in the ground when it is pulled or dug, making it nearly impossible to eradicate without the use of chemicals.

Foamflower

Once a very popular groundcover and woodland garden plant, **foamflower**, *Tiarella cordifolia*, has been passed over to a certain degree by its showier cousins the coralbells, whose brightly colored leaves are more eye-catching on the garden center shelf. For shady, woodland conditions, though, few groundcovers are as successful as foamflower. Spreading rather quickly to form large masses, they'll cover the ground in a season or two, and while they are technically deciduous, they will frequently maintain some foliage through at least part of the winter. As with coralbells, tremendous advances in breeding over the past two decades have completely transformed the foamflower into a plant that in some cases is almost unrecognizable when compared to the simple green woodland dweller it once was. Recent crosses between the spreading foamflower and brightly colored coralbells have yielded spreading plants with brightly colored leaves, hybrids called **Heucherella**, that combine the finest attributes of both parents. For a bright splash of color in the shade garden, *Tiarella* and *Heucherella* can't be beat.

■ Tiarella is a **native groundcover** for the shade garden. Recent hybrids between it and coralbells have yielded colorful plants with spreading habits. White or pink flowers appear for up to six weeks in spring and may be very showy on newer hybrids.
■ **PART SHADE TO SHADE.** ■ **ZONES 3 TO 8.**

Green-and-Gold

A semievergreen groundcover, **green-and-gold**, *Chrysogonum virginianum* (also called goldenstar), is an excellent native alternative to some of our more invasive, nonnative groundcovers. Growing just a few inches tall, it will spread nicely to cover open ground, but work its way around nearby plants rather than running over or through them. Its golden yellow, daisylike blooms are borne profusely in spring and early summer against dark green foliage. Flowering continues sporadically throughout the summer and picks up again as cooler autumn weather settles in. It may be completely deciduous in the coldest part of its hardiness range, but it will quickly emerge in spring as the weather warms, often flowering at the same time it is producing new growth.

Several selections have been made over the years, including forms with improved disease resistance, longer season of bloom and improved growth habit. **'Allen Bush'** is an improved form noted for its compact habit and exceptional spring floral display. **'Eco Lacquered Spider'** was introduced by plantsman Don Jacobs of Eco Gardens in Decatur, Georgia, and features glossy green leaves and unusually long, purple runners by which the plant spreads.

■ Green-and-gold is an excellent native groundcover for shady areas and is also **useful in rain gardens** or along the edges of woodland paths. It has a long bloom season, flowering from April through June and again in autumn as the weather cools. ■ **PART SHADE TO SHADE.** ■ **ZONES 5 TO 8.**

Resources

Hardiness Zone Map

USDA Plant Hardiness Zone Map
http://planthardiness.ars.usda.gov/PHZMWeb/

Books

Armitage, Allan M. *Herbaceous Perennial Plants*,
2nd edition. Champaign, IL: Stipes Publishing, 1997.

Brookes, John. *Garden Masterclass*. New York:
Dorling Kindersley Publishers, 2002.

Clausen, Ruth Rogers. *Perennials for American
Gardens*. New York: Random House, 1989.

Dirr, Michael A. *Manual of Woody Landscape Plants*.
Champaign, IL: Stipes Publishing, 1998.

DiSabato-Aust, Tracy. *The Well-Tended Perennial
Garden*. Portland, OR: Timber Press, 2006.

Online Resources

National Gardening Association
www.garden.org

Fine Gardening Magazine Online
www.finegardening.com

Rodale's Organic Gardening
www.organicgardening.com

Index